EAST
toward
DAWN

A WOMAN'S SOLO JOURNEY AROUND THE WORLD

Nan Watkins

SEAL PRESS

EAST TOWARD DAWN
A WOMAN'S SOLO JOURNEY AROUND THE WORLD

Seal Press
An Imprint of Avalon Publishing Group Inc.
161 William St., 16th Floor
New York, NY 10038

First Seal Press edition 2002

Grateful acknowledgement is made for the use of an excerpt from Emily Dickinson's "Some keep the Sabbath," reprinted by permission of the publishers and the Trustees of Amherst College from *The Poems of Emily Dickinson,* Thomas H. Johnson, ed., Cambridge, Mass.: The Belknap Press of Harvard University Press, Copyright © 1951, 1955, 1979 by the President and Fellows of Harvard College; and for the use of an excerpt from Lorine Niedecker's "Wintergreen Ridge," reprinted by permission of the Estate of Lorine Niedecker, Cid Corman, executor, from *The Granite Pail: The Selected Poems of Lorine Niedecker,* Cid Corman, ed., Frankfort, Kentucky: Gnomon Press, Copyright © 1996.

Library of Congress Cataloging-in-Publication Data is available.

ISBN: 1-58005-064-6

Printed in the United States of America
Distributed by Publishers Group West

Contents

Acknowledgments

The journey that led to writing this book began at a gathering of women classmates from George School when I talked with Jean Gould about the trips we had each taken to Nepal. A year later, I answered her call for submissions for an anthology of women's writing, which she was preparing for Seal Press. I owe great thanks to Jean for opening the door to the world of travel writing and for continuing to steer me in positive directions. Jennie Goode was the editor at Seal Press who asked if I would be interested in writing a book-length account of my solo trip around the world. I am grateful to Jennie for setting me on the path and helping me sort my initial thoughts about my odyssey.

Faith Conlon took over as my editor and mentor when Jennie left. My gratitude to Faith for her timely suggestions, patience and expert guidance in helping me turn my rice-paper notes into a travel memoir. I extend my thanks to all on her able team at Seal Press for their good and cheerful service, especially Cathy Johnson, copy editor, and Anne Mathews, managing editor. My thanks, also, to Claiborne Hancock, managing editor at Avalon Publishing Group, for piloting the manuscript into a book. I salute my colleagues at Hunter Library for their readiness to aid in my many requests for help.

During the extended period of writing, I received much support and encouragement from my family. I would like to thank Mary Stanley, Betsy and Paul Thomas, Susan and John Hanna, Marnie and Jim Haines, Dianne Sorensen and David Dawson, Barbara and Bob Kay, and Ellen and Eric Kay for their enthusiasm and good humor in tolerating my divided attention. To Thomas Crowe, who bore the daily demands of living with a preoccupied partner, my special thanks for his inspiration, fortitude, gourmet meals and incisive comments at various stages of my writing.

I could not have undertaken my round-the-world journey without the financial help of William and Rani Aldis and Norman and Lyn Dawson; my unending thanks for their goodwill and generous support. I offer my heartfelt appreciation to Ann and Lou Sica, John Gorman, Barbara and Jim Demetrion, Jean Kennedy, Helmut and Philine Fuhrmann, Mia and Al Gilman, Anita Oser, Alex Kekesi, Chan and Miegan Gordan, and James and Luke Thompson for their enduring friendship. I treasure the gracious hospitality of my friends around the world who so willingly welcomed me into their homes: Joan and Marie O'Flynn, Wil and Rosemary Rees, Eugen and Friederike Braun, Indira and Jay Pal Shrestha, Nava Raj and Meena Subedi, Dambar and Shanthi Shrestha, Jurme and Namgay Wangchuck. The cordiality of everyone in their households to a wayfaring traveler confirms my belief that we are all kindred souls in one mighty family.

For Ellen

New York
For Travel's Sake

> I travel not to go anywhere, but to go. I travel for
> travel's sake. The great affair is to move.
>
> —Robert Louis Stevenson,
> *Travels with a Donkey*

Surfacing from the subway into the brilliant lights of Times Square, I feel the shock of arrival at the quick-silver hub of America's most energetic city. It is a November evening, just after dinner and before the theater, and the huge square is packed with people and vehicles of every description.

I try to absorb the rich color and variety of the scene—the giant neon signs emblazoning the names of corporate America: Coca-Cola, Eight O'Clock Bean Coffee, Hertz, AT&T; the tall buildings with windows alight far above me; the flashing signs assaulting my eyes. In the river of people streaming around me, I see a profuse variety of young and old, rich and poor, thin and hefty, tall and short, black and white. The cacophony of sounds—car horns, bus engines, squealing brakes, steel drum bands, footsteps, foreign languages—is an urban opera to my ears. Times Square is even more bedazzling than I remember it as a child.

I've just come from dinner with my daughter, Ellen, and her fiancé, Eric, in a neighborhood restaurant in Brooklyn. The pungent smells coming from the Lebanese kitchen mingled with the Middle Eastern music swirling through the dining room transported us into a relaxed, weekend mood. Over *kebabs* and *kifta,* I watched Ellen and Eric in the window seat, outlined with small, sparkling white lights, speaking happily about their life in the city. They looked sophisticated and at ease in their new surroundings—quite a contrast from when I last saw them in casual summer wear, posing for pictures on the lawn of my home in the Blue Ridge Mountains.

I'm on the road again, and it feels exciting to be starting my travels in this intense metropolis that has served as destination for countless people from all over the globe. I wanted the first stop on my journey to be with my daughter, who serves as a touchstone in my life. After dinner, Eric went off to play saxophone at one of his gigs, leaving mother and daughter to spend the evening together. She and I have come to Broadway to see a new show called *Art.*

We turn down West Forty-fifth Street, the fall wind ruffling our hair. Ellen, in her chic chocolate-brown leather jacket, forges her way through throngs of New Yorkers seeking entertainment on a Saturday night. We approach the marquee of the Royale Theatre, ablaze with more lights than my entire North Carolina town. We move inside and are enveloped in the deep-red fabric of the theater. We find our balcony seats and settle in for an evening of dramatic surprises. As the lights dim, I feel the familiar warmth of my daughter's arm on the armrest we share. The curtains part, and the play begins.

When I first had the idea of celebrating my sixtieth birthday by traveling solo around the world, I was intrigued to hear the responses of my family and friends. Thomas, the man with whom I share my life, was both encouraging and discouraging, wanting me to be free to follow my dream, yet worrying I might not want to return home after seeing so much of the world. My friend Mia, who loves the adventure of travel as much as I do, wholeheartedly urged me to go. My two sisters and cousin were supportive, but fretted about my taking such an extensive trip alone. Would I be safe? Would I be happy traveling by myself? One evening, my youngest sister, Susan, chirped into the phone, "I love you, but I think you're crazy!"

In the days when I was considering the trip, I couldn't help thinking of what my son, Peter, would say, if he were alive. Peter was in harmony with his world and had the knack of making a strange place feel like home. That was something I hoped to achieve on my journey. I knew Peter would approve.

Perhaps I was happiest that my daughter was strongly encouraging. Moving beyond the years of her childhood and youth, Ellen and I have forged a relationship as two adult women and have become good friends. Over the preceding months she continued to prod me gently, making sure I remained on target for the trip.

Finally, after considering all advice and receiving generous financial gifts from family and loyal friends, I committed my own small savings and took the plunge. I sketched a plan to travel around the world for sixty days, celebrating the sixty years of my life.

When three travel agencies failed to reply to my inquiries, I decided to make all the travel arrangements myself. I began contacting airlines, trying to patch together a trip, until one helpful woman suggested I call the "round-the-world desk." I learned that airlines offer, for a flat rate, round-the-world tickets valid for a year of travel to destinations within their flight routes, as long as the travel is in one direction, either east or west. I decided to travel east toward the dawn.

Even as a girl, I loved the process of traveling to new places. Whether plane or train, bicycle or boat, camel or my own two feet, I love the various modes of travel. Like Robert Louis Stevenson, I love "to go." I like the challenge of making my way around a new town for the first time, of talking to strangers, with whom I can exchange a few intimate thoughts and then move on.

I have often dreamed of circling the earth, of feeling the roundness of the planet, the wholeness of the sphere. I like the idea of traveling in one direction until I'm back where I started, of moving forward every step of the way, as in the journey of life itself. I relish the challenge of being out in the world on my own, of circling the globe at a leisurely pace, enjoying my inner journey as much as my outward one.

I contemplate what lies ahead: the cold rain of northern Europe, the austere beauty of the Himalaya, the jungles of southern Nepal, the grandeur of maharajas' palaces, the camel carts of Rajasthan, the ricksha drivers of Bangladesh, the tidy little country of Singapore, the balmy paradise of the Big Island of Hawaii. I wonder where in India I'll be on December 18, my sixtieth birthday.

Feeling lucky to be in New York just after the opening of the monumental Jackson Pollock retrospective, I spend Sunday afternoon viewing the exhibition in the Museum of Modern Art. At the entrance, I am immediately drawn to the small self-portrait of the artist as a young man. Its round brown countenance bears a startled and questioning look; the dark eyes emanate from a worn mask of a face. I see from the label by the portrait that Pollock was in his early twenties when he painted the canvas. He began his life as an artist at the same age my son died.

I take the long walk through the galleries filled with Pollock's work, a witness to his inner life expressed in paint. Past his student work, his sketches, and then moving on to the paintings originating in myth, I watch as the brush strokes in the early pictures gradually give way to experiments of dripping paint on canvas, then poured liquid lines. I am overcome by the size of Pollock's later works. The huge canvases had been stretched out on the floor of Pollock's studio, so that he could move around all four sides, using his entire body, like a dancer, to fill the space with paint. The paintings are a written record of his impassioned dance: *Lavender Mist, Autumn Rhythm, Convergence.*

The last masterpiece of the exhibition, *Blue Poles*, takes my breath away. It is a giant canvas so densely smothered with poured lines, thick and thin, dark and light, that Pollock had to add eight blue poles to steady himself, to keep from losing his way in the jungle of paint. It's as if Pollock were trying to cram his whole life onto one canvas. I am transfixed, lost in his private world, and to keep my balance I hold on tight—to his blue poles.

After the work of the large poured canvases, I am surprised to find that the artist's energy, his inspiration, appear to have given out, as if he had lost his way. The last paintings are the work of a man without direction, yet still seeking, as indicated by the title of the final painting, *Search.*

As I walk back through the exhibition, returning to the self-portrait at the beginning, I see the arc of the artist's life as revealed in his work: from the haunting mask-face of the boy barely man, through the explorations of timeless myth and the turbulent depths of his inner self, through the great masterworks of his maturity, to the final loss of and search for direction.

I pause at the entrance to the exhibition and think of myself embarking on a passage around the world. At my journey's end, will I be able to see the arc of my life as clearly as I have seen Pollock's just now? Will I be able to stand back, at sixty, and see the path my life has taken?

• • •

Monday morning the air is brisk and clear. After a pleasant break-fast shared with a couple from Northern Ireland staying at the same bed-and-breakfast, I set out on foot through the streets of Brooklyn Heights. I find Ellen finishing her wake-up coffee in her postage-stamp-size apartment, sharing the morning hour with Bismarck, her faithful cat. Greeting me with a daughter's smile, Ellen slings her miniature leather purse over her shoulder and leads the way out onto the quiet, tree-lined street.

We walk at a good clip, along the famous Promenade, through a neighborhood park and up the steps onto the Brooklyn Bridge, the intricate geometry of the support wires standing out clearly against the morning-blue sky. The pedestrian walkway is considerably above the bridge roadway, so I feel high and free in the open air over the East River. The wind is grand and blustery, and Manhattan shines brightly as the sun glistens off the glass and metal skyline.

I love these fleeting moments with my daughter. I like seeing her as an adult who has established her own life in this cosmopolitan city. When I look at her, I can still see the face of the beautiful child who was once so close to me, both physically and emotionally, that we seemed inseparable. Everywhere I went in those early days, she was with me, sitting happily astride my right hip, viewing the world from a safe height. She needed me then, as I needed her. When she first left the security of home for preschool, I felt an emptiness, as if a part of me—that sweet young girl-child who had accompanied me everywhere—had been torn away. But the lesson of mothers is surrender, of gradually releasing, day by day, the lives of our children, once an integral part of our body, to their own lib-erty. Success is seeing my daughter a mature woman on her own.

Ellen and I traverse the gentle arc of the bridge, pausing to admire the boats on the river, the great height of the twin towers of the World Trade Center. I snap a picture of her, and she returns the favor. We talk about little things, things that neither of us will remember tomorrow. But what we will remember is being together, walking the Brooklyn Bridge on this bright fall day.

When we reach Broadway, Ellen says she's heading for Ellen's Café, her favorite spot for breakfast on her way to work. Before she leaves, she deftly hails a cab for me to take to Kennedy Airport, from where I'll begin the next leg of my journey. What remains in my mind as the cab pulls away from the curb is the smiling face, the glistening dark brown hair, the sparkling eyes of my daughter, now my only child, waving good-bye. I am on my way.

Munich
The City as Muse

> The purpose of life is life itself.
> —Johann Wolfgang von Goethe,
> Letter to Heinrich Meyer

I was just sixteen when I took my first giant step: in June 1955, I boarded an old steamship and set out without my family for a three-month stay in Europe. I had to set sail from Quebec, because the *Arosa Kulm,* which had been sunk twice, did not pass the safety standards of the New York Port Authority. To my teenage eyes the ship looked terrific. My father, eager to see his eldest daughter make her way in the world, encouraged me strongly in my bold adventure, but I remember my mother struggling to stifle her anxiety about my sailing on such a risky vessel. Clutching my copy of Kipling's "If," which I had memorized as a kind of creed to help me through the rough spots (though I changed the last line to the unpoetic "You'll be a woman, my daughter"), I waved good-bye to my family from the rail of that rusty, if not trusty, old student ship and began the ten-day crossing of the Atlantic.

Those three months in Europe gave me my initial contact with another culture, and, just as important, with a nation of people who had recently been "the enemy." For most of the summer I served in a work camp sponsored by the American Friends Service Committee in the postwar West Zone of Germany. Our project was to

begin building a foundation and house for boys who had lost both
parents during World War II. We student volunteers from three
schools—George School, my Quaker school in Pennsylvania, and
our two affiliated schools in Germany—lived with the orphaned
boys in rudimentary, unheated barracks, sleeping in bunk beds and
washing ourselves in cold water with the luxury of one quick, hot
shower per week. We rose each morning at six o'clock, assembled
for Quaker Meeting in a cold stone building, struggling to keep our
eyes open, and were hard at work by eight o'clock. The language
spoken was German, which I had studied for two years.

By the time the summer was over, I felt a real sense of accom-
plishment. I had worked in "the pit," excavating stone for the foundation of the house. I had pushed wheelbarrows of that stone to the
site for the house, peeled hundreds of potatoes I helped dig from the
garden, and washed the camp laundry, stirring the clothes with a
wooden paddle in a huge vat of boiling water over a fire we had
built. I had played an upright piano in a duel of Beethoven sonatas
with Willi, a blonde, blue-eyed orphan, who amazed me by being
as good at playing soccer as he was at playing Beethoven. I had
dated—for the first time—a German boy named Josef, whose eyes
were as dark as mine and who gave me a not-quite-gold locket on
our last night together when we walked arm in arm through the
moonlit fields. I had smoked my first—and last—cigarette, a bitter
Russian brand bought by the boys just over the border in the East
Zone. And I regularly drank a bottle of beer with my dinner of a
whole smoked fish and potatoes and fresh greens from the garden.
I ended each meal with a cup of *ersatzkaffee,* a "substitute" coffee
made from barley because of the scarcity of coffee beans. The most
important thing I learned that summer was that people everywhere
share the same human desire for a good life; outwardly we may
differ and even come to blows as enemies, but inwardly we share
similar hopes and fears and dreams.

Our little troop of eight American students and two chaperons eventually said an emotional farewell to the orphan boys and began a tour that took us to the host schools in Düsseldorf and Berlin, where we each stayed with a German family. I took my first airplane ride, from Hanover to Berlin, as the East Zone of Germany, under Communist control, was closed to foreign travelers. I still remember eating dinner with my host family in Berlin. The father served two pork chops for the five of us at the table. Despite my embarrassed protests, I was given one chop, while the other was divided four ways between the parents and children. It was the parents' way of showing their highest form of hospitality. My German "sisters" were great company and took me all over the bombed-out city of West Berlin by streetcar, chiding me not to fall asleep while riding, lest I end up behind the Iron Curtain in Soviet East Berlin. I remember the hollow feeling in my stomach when I saw the churches, public buildings and apartment houses that American bombs had destroyed.

One afternoon in Berlin I met a German girl named Christie, who, like myself, was a pianist. She took me to her school auditorium, where a grand piano sat on the stage. I asked her to play for me, and she agreed, if I would play for her. She performed beautifully, I thought, and then I sat down at the piano. When I finished playing some Bach and Schubert, she looked at me, pale and dazed. "I'll never play for you again," she said. "Why didn't you tell me you played so well?" It was my turn to be shocked. I told her I was a student, just like her, and encouraged her the best way I knew how. There were few people I could talk to seriously about my music, and I wanted to continue the exchange with Christie. But Christie kept her word: she never played for me again, even when she came to the United States and lived with my family for a year while attending my high school.

After flying out of Berlin, we Americans took the train through Switzerland to Paris, where we stayed in a sixth floor walk-up and played tourists in the city for a week, seeing the floor show at the Moulin Rouge and eating all the French bread and pastries we could find. We finally boarded the *Arosa Kulm* in Le Havre and made the return voyage to Quebec. My mother was waiting on the dock in joyous relief at my return. But I had been hooked by travel. My first words to my family were "I want to go back."

The heavy rain on the autobahn is no hindrance for Friederike Braun, who steps on the accelerator of her little car and speeds down the open highway. My eyes gravitate to the speedometer, which registers an eye-popping 145 kilometers per hour. The sky is a uniform gray, and the Bavarian countryside, drenched with the rains of mid-November, is sodden but clean. I look for signs of the new reunited Germany, but see nothing different on this bleak afternoon.

Rike (pronounced Reeka) is one of the international students who, in the early eighties, studied at Western Carolina University, where I work. I first met her in Germany, years before, through my husband at the time, a professor of German. It was because of him that Rike came to study in the United States, but over the years she and I developed a friendship of our own. A strikingly beautiful woman who is now the mother of three boys and expecting a fourth, Rike is an architect in the midst of realizing her dream of designing and building her own house.

Rike pulls the car into her driveway in a new neighborhood of a small town outside of Munich. Inside, the house is warm and cheerful, and I am quickly welcomed into her lively family. The boys greet me, and I switch back into the German of my student years. Over tea they tell me that tomorrow is Saint Martin's Day, or Martinmas; they bring out a large box of homemade lanterns and ask me to choose which lantern I want to carry in the school parade. Hearing about the holiday reminds me of the many feast days I celebrated as a student in this capital of Germany's largest and predominantly Catholic state.

Saint Martin, born of a simple family in the fourth century in what is now Hungary, became the Bishop of Tours. He is remembered as a kind and compassionate man who once leapt from his horse and split his cloak in two with his sword so that he could give half of the cloak to a shivering beggar. After his death, his cloak, or *cappa,* was kept in a movable shrine called a *capella.* Our word "chapel" derives from this Latin word. As an ardent Christian, Martin destroyed temples and trees and other sites held sacred by those he termed pagan. Legend says that once, when his enemies were chasing him, he hid among a flock of geese.

Saint Martin's Day dawns with a cold drizzle, a slight wind and an overcast sky. The commotion of four boys bouncing and clowning in the next room wakes me from a sound sleep. As I come out into the hall in my nightgown, I hear a little neighbor boy ask, *"Was macht die alte Frau?"* (What's the old woman doing?) I feel stabbed—the old woman! The German child is seeing me as I was shocked to see myself, two days earlier in Kennedy Airport, looking like old Mother Courage in Brecht's opera, stubbornly pulling her wagon behind her through all the trials of her war-torn life. I had caught a glimpse of myself, pulling my suitcase behind me, my long silver hair trailing down my back, and I couldn't avoid the comparison. I had been surprised to notice how old I looked compared with how young I felt inside. The little boy is seeing only the old exterior.

Over breakfast of crunchy hard rolls, fresh fruit and cheese and green tea in mustard-yellow cups, I ask Rike what she thinks of my long hair. After my divorce, I had decided to let my hair grow long to mark the change in my life, not only an outward change in appearance, but an inward one as well. I was following the traditional belief that long hair, as in the biblical story of Samson, is a source of power.

"You know I always tell the truth," Rike begins, and proceeds to say she had not recognized me at first in the Munich airport because I looked like "some old woman" with long gray hair. "That does it!" I say and, without further hesitation, we drive to Rike's hairdresser, who gives me an excellent short, tapered cut that frames my face. The years fall away as the locks of hair fall to the floor. "Ten years younger," Rike says. And with the ease of an invalid who no longer needs a crutch, I leave the long silver braids behind.

Evening comes, and I ride to the Montessori school with the boys for the Saint Martin's Day celebration, while Rike joins her husband to check on their new house. I take my goose lantern, and Philip, the eldest son, lights the candle inside. As the flame from the match flares, I watch Philip's handsome face closely, for he was born eight days after my son, Peter, died. The hour of Philip's birth coincided to the minute with the hour of Peter's birth twenty-two years earlier. It is as if, Rike and I sometimes say, my son's spirit has continued in her son, and this bond has made Rike's and my friendship even stronger. We remember that week of death and birth as the tenderest mingling of sorrow and joy.

I set out in the parade holding four-year-old Hendrik's chubby hand, walking in the cold wind and drizzle and talking in German with mothers and fathers of the other children. We march through an open meadow along a creek and eventually assemble, huddling our bright lanterns together in the darkness, while the ruddy-faced children sing in their sweet voices one folk-song after another about Saint Martin hiding among the geese and giving his cloak to a beggar.

How easy it has been for me to leave home and move out into the world! In a matter of hours, I am completely immersed in the life of this German community. Watching Moritz's seven-year-old earnestness as he sings and holding Hendrik's warm hand, I feel immediately connected to this place, this crowd of people I have never met before. Stamping my feet to warm them against the November chill, I walk back through the Bavarian meadow to the school, where hot apple cider and goose-shaped sugar cookies are served. I watch a young father supervise the bonfire, and eager children stand as close as they can, poking their sticks into the fire. I hear the rain hiss as it falls into the glowing embers.

Old Munich, which I love so much, is today a prosperous, attractive and complex modern city thriving in its favorable location at the foot of the Bavarian Alps. It is the most popular city in Germany for both German and foreign visitors, and its university is the most sought-after among students. Munich was originally a settlement of monks, and the city's native name——München—comes from the German word for monks, mönche. Munich was founded in 1158, exactly eight hundred years before I arrived to spend my junior year abroad at the university. It survived the bombing of World War II, although its symbol, the twelfth-century cathedral Frauenkirche, or Church of Our Lady, was shattered by Allied bombs. Like many other destroyed architectural masterpieces, it was painstakingly rebuilt after the war. The city is filled with palaces, the largest and most elegant of which is Nymphenburg— my favorite, because the boy Mozart entertained the local royalty

there, astonishing them with his genius at the keyboard. Today
Munich upholds its long history of an active cultural life, and its
reputation as a city for good fun, copious Bavarian beer and sausage
happily continues.

Three years after my work-camp summer in Germany, I set sail
for Europe again, this time to study in Munich. All of my university classes were in German, and I ate, dreamed and dated in
German, so my spoken German improved by leaps and bounds. I
pursued my piano playing with discipline and energy, studying
with two teachers and practicing in tiny soundproof rooms
belonging to the music department. It feels, in retrospect, as if I
grew more in my one student year in Munich than I did in my other
three college years at Oberlin. That year in Munich was my appren-
ticeship to life, my first taste of freedom as a young adult. It was
Munich, the city, that played muse to my spirit in the critical time
when I was emerging into my own.

I remember Munich, back in the fifties, as a city choked with
traffic and overflowing with life, particularly in the fall, when the
world-famous Oktoberfest took place on the Theresa Meadow. In
those days, I took a tram from the neighborhood where I lived,
through the center of town, called Stachus, and then northeast to
the university and the student quarter, Schwabing.

Living in Munich while the city was celebrating its eight hun-
dredth anniversary felt like one long festival to me. I met students
from all over Germany and many other countries of the world. We
played and studied and talked and ate and drank together in
unending combinations of nationalities and points of view. We
went to the opera together, the theater, the puppet shows and the
cabarets, where we stayed late into the night. We sunbathed in the
English Garden, skied and hiked in the Bavarian Alps and drank
as much beer as we could hold in the Hofbräuhaus. I danced many

a night away in the Hungarian refugee community with students who had fled the Soviet crackdown after the uprising of 1956. It was a new experience for me to be intimately involved with a group of political dissidents. The first time I stayed up all night was for one of the fabulous, outrageous costume balls held during Fasching, or Carnival, before Lent.

During the long semester breaks, which seemed to be created for students to get out of the musty lecture halls and experience the real world around them, I traveled across Europe. In the warm summer months I hitchhiked north through Germany, Holland and Belgium, staying in youth hostels for the equivalent of twenty-five cents a night. I joined the other hostelers washing dishes, cooking and sweeping floors to help defray the cost. Trying to hitch a ride on the autobahn, I was picked up by German police in a Porsche, and just when I thought luck had left me, the police cheerfully drove me to a two-lane road where it was legal to hitchhike. I was repeatedly impressed by the way Europeans encouraged their students to get out and see the world, to taste and enjoy their heritage and culture. Being a student in Europe was like being on an extended honeymoon with life.

Over winter break I headed southeast on the Orient Express, traveling through Communist Yugoslavia on an old train pulled by a giant steam-powered locomotive bearing a gold silhouette of Marshal Tito. My destination was Greece, which I embraced as the cradle of my own civilized being. Every step I climbed up to the Acropolis felt like another step toward enlightenment. I gazed in awe at the long rows of slightly inward-tilting Doric columns which rose over the slightly curved base of the white marble skeleton of the Parthenon, giving the structure a bearing and grace I had never beheld before. Perhaps it is so powerful today because it is open to the sky, the Mediterranean air giving breathing space to the superb clarity of design, the way a measure of silence counter-balances the lush sound of a great symphony. I walked among the lofty columns of that venerable temple to the virgin goddess, trying to imagine the huge ivory and gold statue of Athena, goddess of war and peace, wisdom and art, once the focal point of the Parthenon, where the ancient Greeks came to worship.

Walking over the stony white Acropolis under the pure Greek sky, I felt my first personal epiphany, as James Joyce would say. So deeply did the beauty of the architecture on that Grecian hilltop affect me that it changed my idea of what mankind could do. It showed me an ideal, a subtlety of thought I had not known before. It felt wonderfully exciting to awaken to a new level of perception—which is what James Joyce meant when he used the term "epiphany" in his own life. That day on the Acropolis has remained with me, an inspiration for my continuing search, for remaining awake to new possibilities.

After Athens I made my first pilgrimage through the mountains to Delphi, riding a bus over the hairpin-curved roads with motion-sick locals, who threw their barf bags out the open bus windows onto the stubbly, parched earth. I felt instantly at home in Delphi and loved the way the remains of the ancient Temple of Apollo rested securely on a ledge formed by two great crags of mountain, yet overlooked the open valley beyond. No longer visible, but pal-pable in the air, were the words "Know thyself" once inscribed on the temple. I adopted that essential command as a mantra, which I have been contemplating ever since. Thousands of years of history, dating back to the goddess tradition, fill those mountains. It was there that the Delphic oracle, a priestess or crone, breathed intoxi-cating fumes rising from the ground beneath the temple, gaining prophetic powers sought by kings. Part of her ritual was to drink from the sacred Castalian Spring, a small stream of water flowing down Mount Parnassus. Tradition says the spring is the source of creative inspiration. Kneeling on the warm rocks, I, too, performed the ritual of drinking from the Castalian Spring, cupping my hands to bring the fertile water to my lips.

Leaving Greece, I traveled on by boat and train through Italy, France and Spain, nearly missing the train in Marseilles because I was dancing with a fellow traveler I had just met, Barry Goldwater, Jr. He had taken me to a nightclub, where I watched my first striptease, a disappointing show put on by a petite, shy, small-breasted Asian girl for the benefit of sailors from all over the world. Afterwards, we were engrossed in dancing cheek-to-cheek when, like Cinderella, I noticed the time and raced to the railroad station to catch my train to Madrid. When I woke the next morning greeted by the moist ocean air of San Sebastian instead of the dry desert air of Madrid, I knew I had climbed into the wrong car of the train the night before. I wondered if Barry had found his way to Port-Bou on the east coast of Spain, where he was planning to lie on the beach, hippie style, and write his memoir of growing up as the son of a famous conservative senator.

One other important memory from that remarkable year in Munich concerns a woman named Dr. Thea Bach. Luck led me to find a room in her large, inviting apartment at the edge of the meadow where the Oktoberfest is held, and from the moment I stepped into her home, she treated me like a family member and friend. When she learned I was in Munich to study classical music, she personally introduced me to the musical and cultural life of the city. She turned her fine record collection over to me, and I spent hours lying in her living room alcove on a gold velvet cushion, listening to recordings of the greatest European artists of the day. She introduced me to her friend, composer Carl Orff, who took me to observe the Bavarian Radio Symphony Orchestra recording sessions of his opera *Oedipus der Tyrann*. While Orff worked onstage with the other musicians, arranging the novel instruments he had designed himself, I sat alone in a sea of empty seats in the huge concert hall and held my breath when Wolfgang Sawallisch, the conductor, turned to address his audience of one before the recording began with the words, *"Ruhe, bitte."* (Quiet, please.)

Thea Bach, herself a cultured professor of literature, introduced me to writers and young friends and treated me to the best seats in the house to see theater performances of Molière in the Cuvilliés Theater, whose crimson and gold Rococo interior sparkled like jewels. On Christmas Eve she bade me wait until she threw open the double doors to her living room and revealed a celebration of lights, the Christmas tree, or *tannenbaum,* sparkling with flaming candles. And then she invited me to share her Christmas feast.

All through my stay, Thea Bach mentored me in my passion for music and life, and at the end of the year I felt hopelessly inadequate to thank her for her enormous generosity. I told her, with sadness, that I would never be able to repay her. And I still remember her reply. "You won't repay me directly, but you will do things for others, just as I have done for you." With that statement she showed me a path that I have taken—a lifetime of mentoring and friendship with young people, many of whom were foreign students in America, as I had once been in Munich.

The rain is no deterrent to my taking a train from Rike's house into Munich to visit my beloved old city. Stepping out of the railroad station, I immediately see changes from the Munich of my student days. What had once been choked corridors of polluting traffic are now streamlined pedestrian zones. A subway has been built that siphons off the excess car traffic. Parking lots have been added away from city center, and people are encouraged to ride the clean, efficient, punctual commuter trains. I see all this as progress and am relieved that the Germans are reckoning with the issues of increased population, pollution, recycling and mass transit. They are taking the long view and trying to improve the quality of life for themselves and their children.

I walk along avenues of stores expertly stocked with every conceivable commodity. I look for my old favorites: Donisl's, the eating place famous for its many varieties of sausage; Dallmayr's, the gourmet shop with the best coffee in Munich; Hugendubel's, the famous multistoried bookstore opposite the New City Hall. All these are still here, and best of all, in the distance I see the Viktualienmarkt, occupying its central place as the open-air city market, where farmers throughout the region sell their best produce, cheeses and meats. I wander past the colorful stalls and then walk over to Max-Josef-Platz and see for the first time the rebuilt Bavarian National Theater, which had been a bombed-out shell in my student days. I walk down Theatinerstrasse to Ludwigstrasse and on to the university, which looks just as I remember it.

Forty years it has been since I inhabited those walls, sitting or standing in crammed lecture halls, listening to professors spout their knowledge about music, art history and philosophy. Do I remember what they said? No, not the words, but I do remember the spirit of their lectures. I remember the enthusiasm with which they talked of their subjects, and I remember how exhilarating it felt to be living in the midst of the history they were talking about. I remember feeling humbled by how much I didn't know, how much I had to learn.

I remember, too, that here where I am standing on Geschwister-Scholl-Platz, two students who were brother and sister once dared to distribute leaflets against the Nazi Party, for which they were put to death. Keeping their name alive is a chilling reminder of how a people with a great cultural history can succumb to unthinkable horror, just as an individual who has led an exemplary life can commit a capital crime. It is important to recognize that we, too, are fallible, that without constant vigilance, we, too, can falter, as a nation or an individual. No guarantees. Learning the horrors of the Second World War, or any war, is lost on us if we think we are above such acts. Each of us is endowed with the capacity for evil as well as good.

On my last day in Germany, Rike and I take the commuter train to Munich together. We walk past the elegant shops in town and go to the old soup kitchen in the Viktualienmarkt. We order the liver dumpling soup, ladled out steaming hot into big white bowls. We sit in the open air at long wooden tables with other townsfolk, under the trees still dripping from the rain.

I take a bite of the warm liver dumpling and think back wistfully to the many bowls of soup I once ate from this kitchen. I think of the fresh opportunities that were available to me in this city and of the people who made my student days memorable. I'm glad Munich looks so good and that the city is maintaining its tradition of playing muse to the eager students of today. The wise words that Thea Bach spoke to me forty years ago echo in my mind. Just as Thea once hosted me here, I once welcomed Rike in the United States, and she in turn is hosting me now. I like to think we are part of a great chain of friendship that will continue to link people throughout the world, in unique ways, for longer than I can imagine.

Zurich
Dinner with Joyce

> Welcome, O life! I go to encounter for the
> millionth time the reality of experience.
>
> —James Joyce,
> *A Portrait of the Artist as a Young Man*

I have come to this Swiss city for the first time, not for its famous financial center, not for the luxury shopping on the Bahnhofstrasse, but for James Joyce. Here, in Zurich, in this neutral country, Joyce found safe haven from the encroaching dangers of the Second World War and here, by chance, he is buried. I have come to honor my favorite modern writer, the man whose torrent of words on paper so shocked his compatriots that they would not print his masterwork in their country during his lifetime. But I'm removed from all that. Joyce's words simply make me rejoice!

One of the benefits of traveling alone is having the freedom to make all decisions myself, without needing to compromise with companions about how to proceed. Today, despite the heavy November rain, I feel like walking rather than hiring a taxi from the train station to my hotel. Adjusting the wool hat I bought in Munich to protect me from the worst of the rain—I don't travel with an umbrella anymore—I cross the tram tracks and the bridge over the Limmat River, which originates in Lake Zurich and flows through the center of town. The rain is falling in sheets, and I'm just able to make out the ducks and swans moving about in the water below. The clouds are much too dense for me to see the Alps beyond.

I find my small, family-run hotel easily, and my first test is to figure out how to open the door. There's no handle in sight, and I'm unable to push the glass door open. Then I notice a button to the right of the entrance, and when I push it, the door folds open, accordion-style, just long enough for me to slip inside.

I am pleased to learn that the reservation I made on the Internet, a first for me, is in good order. I am given two keys, each of which—like the entrance door—requires figuring out. I feel like the young girl in the fairy tale who must solve a riddle to advance to the next room. I climb the stairs, at each floor pushing a power-saving light switch that stays lit just long enough for me to walk through. I finally reach my room and unlock the door to find an inviting bed with a pristine white linen cover over a fluffy *federbett* (goose down comforter). My window overlooks the back street, and I can hear a man singing and women talking in the rain.

I want to make the most of my time here, so I collect my thoughts and, checking to see that my city map is close at hand, I set out in the pouring rain to buy two red roses to put on the grave of Joyce and his wife, Nora. With my flowers carefully wrapped, I walk back through the rain to the nearest tram stop and take shelter under the small roof on the platform.

Unlike my student days in Munich years ago, there is no conductor to take fares and give tickets and directions on the tram. I find the automat, which people are stoking with Swiss francs, but even after studying the listed fares, I can't figure out what to do. So, in German, I ask an elderly woman where the zoo is. I once read that Joyce's wife had commented after his funeral that she thought he would like the cemetery because it was near the zoo, where he could hear his beloved lions roar.

"You must realize that this is not a good day to visit the zoo," the woman replies in the Zurich German dialect, her voice raised so that I can hear her above the heavy rain. I explain that I am really looking for the Fluntern Cemetery, and she nods understandingly when she sees the flowers. She patiently tells me I need to go to the end of Line 6, and with some juggling to get the right change to pay the fare, I purchase my round-trip ticket to the zoo.

With a feeling of relief, even comfort, I sit back in the warm, dry tram car, which slowly makes its way around the curves and up the hill. I see the buildings of the University of Zurich and ride through the quiet middle-class neighborhood of tree-lined streets where James and Nora Joyce once lived. I enjoy the smooth, gliding ride and listen to the rasping sound of the wheels making difficult turns in the track.

When we reach the end of the line at the top of the hill, I disembark and see the entrance to the zoo across the street and, figuring the cemetery must be close by, I head for an area of tall trees on the left. I walk through the iron entrance gate of Friedhof Fluntern and notice signs saying that all flowers must be handed in at the administration building. I hesitate. I have not come these thousands of miles to honor Joyce by giving my roses to a cemetery administrator, so I walk on. I have no idea where Joyce's grave is in this huge place and am reluctant to ask because of my contraband roses. I am amazed at how beautiful the grounds are—they feel more like a park than a cemetery. I walk up the gentle slope that crosses avenue after avenue of neatly tended graves bordered by little hedges and tastefully planted bushes. I decide I will find the gravesite myself if I have to walk until dark.

I meander a long while over gravel pathways. At last I reach a cross-path at the top of the hill and a very small wooden sign that says Joyce and Canetti Graves. My heart leaps. A few more turns and I walk the last steps over glistening wet flagstones to a grassy plot. The grave is covered by a large rectangle of polished black marble, lying flat upon the ground, surrounded by a miniature trimmed boxwood hedge. Four names, outlined in white, are carved into the black stone: James Joyce and Nora Barnacle Joyce, and the names of their son and daughter-in-law. A family headed by the man whose masterpiece, *Ulysses,* changed the course of creative writing in our time, and next to him his wife, his helpmeet, who mastered the practical necessities of life so that her husband could write.

What captivates me is the setting of the grave, with the near life-size statue of Joyce sitting on a bench, walking stick at rest, head cocked slightly to the side, observing the scene through his bronze spectacles. I am relieved to find Joyce's final resting place utterly peaceful, for in his artist's unsettled life of exile he was constantly uprooted. Above the grave, tall hemlocks sway gracefully in the wind and white birches stand guard on the hill. I unwrap my two roses, stash the paper in my bag and lay the red flowers on the black stone. Offerings. To James Joyce for the unflagging spirit that kept him writing, and to Nora for her devotion and enduring love.

I stay here, ignoring the cold and the wet. The last time I visited my mother's grave, it was a rainy day, just like this. The gray marble of her small stone marker, nestled below the gravestone of her parents, was also adorned with wet leaves. I wonder what elixir of love kept James and Nora together through the thick and thin of life, whereas not only my parents, but my husband and I divorced.

"May we ever and ever be very divinely in love" were words I found in a letter my father had written to my mother in the 1930s, before their marriage. A short time later my mother replied, "My last day of teaching tomorrow. I have fewer regrets than I expected. It's just one more proof of my love for you, dear heart, that I can renounce so lightly what has been life itself for me for almost ten years." Despite that loving start, thirty years later my parents' marriage split asunder, and now they lie alone in separate graves.

Unwittingly, I repeated the pattern of my parents and divorced, also after thirty years. Like them, my husband and I had an auspicious beginning. We took a year-long honeymoon in Vienna, where my husband used his Fulbright grant to research his dissertation and I studied piano at the Vienna Academy of Music, learning to play Mozart sonatas as Mozart once played them. Our happiest times together were spent sharing our love of travel, literature and music. We saw and heard von Karajan direct Richard Wagner's monumental cycle, *Der Ring des Nibelungen,* at the Vienna State Opera; we took a tram up into the Vienna Woods to drink the new harvest of wine; my husband drove our miniature Steyr-Puch over the Alps to Venice, where we rode gondolas in the winding canals, and on to Ravenna, where we stood honoring the grave of Dante, who lies there in exile from his native Florence.

The early years of our marriage were full of hope and plans for braiding the strands of our individual lives into a strong and vibrant union. Each of us had an enduring sense of service, and our optimism fueled our desire to make the world a better place. Yet despite the most hopeful beginnings, my husband and I also eventually went our separate ways.

I listen for the lions' roar in the zoo across the way, but all I hear is rain falling through the trees. I walk further down the flagstone path to discover the grave of Elias Canetti, Nobel laureate, another creative writer, another exile. His grave is a rough slab of white marble with his signature carved into the stone; golden birch leaves from the trees above are its only decoration.

I am glad these two sorcerers of words, Joyce and Canetti, share this ancient Swiss hilltop in their eternal rest. I imagine their spirits in witty conversation in the dark nights on this quiet knoll, the same way I think of my mother conversing happily with her Welsh relatives on the hillside above the old coal mine in Pennsylvania. It is a comfort for our earthly minds to believe we can still communicate in death with our beloved, through the spirit.

It is six o'clock in the evening and I have just awoken from a deep sleep. It takes a moment for me to get my bearings under the warm down comforter, but I realize quickly that if I want to eat dinner at the famous Kronenhalle restaurant without a reservation, I had better get going.

With great determination, I set out into the Zurich night. The rain is falling more heavily than ever as I walk along the river, whose waves sparkle with the reflections of city lights. The wind is blowing so hard I have to hold on to my hat. On the way to the restaurant I pass the Café Odéon, which had been a gathering place for artists and exiles like Joyce and Lenin, and I wonder if they ever met each other there. By now I have memorized the central portion of the Zurich map, and I know I have to walk all the way down to the Quai Bridge at the head of Lake Zurich, and at that intersection I will find the restaurant.

One miserably cold and wet January night in 1941, Joyce was feeling ill and depressed, and he decided he wanted to leave his apartment and have dinner at the Kronenhalle. Nora tried her best to dissuade him from going out into the wintry night, but Joyce prevailed. The two ordered a taxi and rode through the blustery dark to the Kronenhalle, where they climbed the flight of stairs to this most hospitable of Swiss restaurants. After enjoying a splendid meal, the Joyces returned home. In the middle of the night Joyce awoke in great pain and was taken to the hospital, where he died of a perforated ulcer. The meal at the Kronenhalle was Joyce's last.

I climb the same flight of stairs the Joyces mounted some fifty years before. Inside the dark wooden double doors, I am greeted with a concerned and questioning look from the maître d'. It's just as well I can't see myself, because I must look a mess. The maître d' inquires if I have a reservation, and in my best German I explain that I am visiting in town and hope very much that he has a free table for me. After a brief consultation with his charts, he beckons me forward and cordially leads me to a waiter standing by a cloak-room, ready to take my soaking coat and hat. I remove my steamed glasses and, after wiping them on my new Swiss linen handker-chief, I replace them to see tall, paneled walls filled profusely with paintings by Picasso, Chagall, Braque and many other twentieth-century artists. The dining room is humming softly with voices in conversation. My waiter, whom I take to be Swiss Italian, shows me to a table with a white linen cloth set impeccably for one. The thought crosses my mind that perhaps he knew all along that I was coming.

Now I know why Joyce loved this place. He had been a friend of the owner, Frau Zumsteg, who hosted artists living in Zurich from 1921 until her death in 1985. She was an art collector and made her restaurant a gathering place for creative people from all parts of Europe. The maître d' is her son.

The waiter exhibits all the traits of first-class European service. He brings the menu, which features a reproduction of a 1972 painting Chagall dedicated to Frau Zumsteg. He carefully takes my order for the house specialty, *Kalbfleisch Geschnezeltes nach Kronen-haller Art,* then asks what wine I would like. I choose a quarter liter of Beaujolais and sit back to enjoy the ambience of this handsome place. The white roll arrives as crusty as it can be; the butter is sweet Swiss butter. The waiter brings a bottle of Swiss mineral water and pours the wine from a small glass pitcher with a mark delineating exactly a quarter of a liter. I raise the delicate goblet to my lips and drink. Just to the left of my table is a Chagall painting: in a snowy night, a grandfather clock is chasing a group of children through a village street while the moon hovers in the blue-black sky.

The art of dining alone is underrated. Without the need to converse with a companion, the single diner can be attentive to the fine food and surroundings and can allow her mind to wander where it will. The pumpkin soup—the perfect texture and temperature—warms my heart. The tender veal in a tasty cream sauce with succulent pan-fried potatoes, Swiss style, brings back intimate memories of wintry evenings: of green velvet curtains; of a grand piano; of watching, from a second-floor window at twilight, an old Viennese woman sweep snow from the pavement with a broom of twigs.

I look at the paintings on the walls and eavesdrop on the conversations of the couples around me. I imagine James and Nora Joyce sitting at one of the tables, enjoying a meal like mine. Joyce would take a bottle of wine with his dinner and lean his head a bit to the side to listen to the talk around him. Nora would look fetching, the neckline of her dark dress low enough to reveal her smooth Irish skin. They would talk little to each other, not needing words for understanding, just a close and familiar silence. They would stay as long as they could in the warmth and ambience of the restaurant, before heading back out into the cold.

I think of the role of the artist in society, of how the artist stands outside the mainstream, exiled as recorder of human experience, critic of human behavior, town crier, visionary. James Joyce was all of these. His masterpiece, *Ulysses,* is the story of a journey, a day in the life of a man in Dublin, but told with such richness, such texture of memory, tradition, experience, forethought, that it is the modern counterpart of *The Odyssey,* the Greek epic told thousands of years ago by Homer. No matter when, no matter where, each of us is on a journey, day by day, year by year, whether we are conscious of it or not. The artist's journey is purposeful; the artist may not be a tidy citizen, but the artist knows why he or she is here: to tell a story, to awaken our minds and hearts to the bigger story of the universe beyond. I admire the artist, who with heightened ability of expression is able to articulate the pain and joy of the human journey through writing, painting, sculpture or music.

In this later stage of my life, I find I, too, want to record the important moments of my journey in my music and writing. My appetite for life has not diminished, and I enjoy as much as ever my interaction with the diverse people I meet along the way. Hobnobbing with the great artists who have gone before me by immersing myself in their works of literature, art and music inspires me to keep plying my own modest form of art.

I finish my dinner of veal and potatoes, and just as I put down my fork, the waiter, who has been watching me attentively from a distance, brings a second serving, identical to the first. He smiles sweetly as he removes the empty plate and sets the full plate before me. I still have a good glass of wine left. I decide if I take my time, I can eat the second serving as well as the first. So I do. And the grandfather clock keeps chasing the children through the dark and snowy street, and the moon continues to light the way.

Airborne
Riding the Wind

Time let me play and be
Golden in the mercy of his means.
—Dylan Thomas, "Fern Hill"

At thirty-five thousand feet above the Black Sea, the orange rays of sunset streak across the sky, shimmering above the deep black bowl of water far below. Pinks and corals tinge the puffs of clouds floating on the horizon. I am in a dreamscape of time and space far from the earthly domain of human activity. I am riding the wind above the great land mass of Eurasia.

It feels like a miracle to be moving at high speed calmly and surely through the air. The wind outside the plane must be of huge magnitude. All the great winds of the world have names—in many cultures winds were gods. Is it Zephyr, the West Wind, who is carrying me now? I relate to the wind not just as the movement of air across the surface of the earth, but also as the element that represents the living spirit, the breath of God. My closest kin among the elements is the wind—the natural force that inspires me with its ever-changing direction, strength, mood.

As a girl I loved walking the windy beaches of Barnegat Bay and Nantucket; as a student one Fourth of July, above the immense Rhone Glacier, I raised my homemade American flag and watched it flap wildly in the wind; as a passionate traveler, I stood for hours on the decks of steamships crossing the Atlantic—in daylight and dark, in calm and in storm—drinking in the wind.

It was some five years ago, after I had been living alone for two years in a little white house in the Blue Ridge Mountains, that I yearned to resume my lifelong affair with the wind. I wanted to return to Wales, the land of my ancestors, and to explore the west coast of Ireland, where the winds howl along the beaches and across the cliffs. Ireland and Wales are excellent places to be if you love the wind. Situated on islands in the North Atlantic, they receive the full force of the westerlies, their wildness untamed from the ocean's expanse. To satisfy my longing for the wind, I booked a flight and alerted friends in Ireland and Wales that I was heading their way.

I landed in Dublin and was greeted by the cheerful smile of Joan O'Flynn, a young Irish friend who had once lived near me in North Carolina. I arrived on a "soft day," she told me, humid with a gray drizzle in the air. Within minutes we were driving south toward Dublin, where we were soon swallowed up in the traffic of daily life. My spirit quickened to be back in James Joyce's town, and before the day was over, I had walked to Joyce's birthplace, a respectable row house a few blocks from where Joan lived. Joyce didn't spend much of his childhood there, for his family had a pattern of moving from place to place, their fortune falling as they grew in numbers, but I was glad to have seen the patch of earth where Joyce had begun his own earthly odyssey.

Early the next morning, Joan and I left Dublin in her car and headed west for the windy coast and County Clare. We ducked over the border into County Galway to visit Thoor Ballylee, Yeats's sixteenth-century tower, where my long hair was once again wrecked by the wind on top of the battlements, and then we set out again for our destination: the Burren. The name means "Great Rock," and that's what I found: a large, desolate stretch of bare limestone, a plateau occupying a vast area in north Clare and strewn with hundreds of stone forts and megalithic tombs. Joan had told me about the place before we arrived, quoting Cromwell's lieutenant-general's description: "Savage land, yielding neither water enough to drown a man, nor a tree to hang him, nor soil enough to bury him."

I couldn't help noticing that this wasteland of rock was carefully defined by stone walls, as if it had been, at one time, valuable grazing land. Joan said the walls were an example of government relief during the Great Potato Famine of the 1840s. During those desperate days, starving citizens were given employment, building unneeded stone walls and roads leading nowhere, in exchange for a pittance of rations. As for Joan, she came to the Burren to see the great array of wildflowers that bloomed in the fissures and deep cracks of the limestone shelf.

Taking advice from a local woman, we followed "the green road," an unpaved lane named for the green grass that had grown up in the center. We bounced along in Joan's Vauxhall until we thought the transmission would fall out and, finally, were forced to a halt near an old stone croft at a curve in the road that had become totally green. I got out of the car and started to walk. I wanted to see what lay ahead. A few hundred yards down the path, I came upon a protected valley carpeted with a brilliant display of wild-flowers. The diffuse light coming through the clouds deepened the color of the flowers. A tall wall made of gray limestone and riddled with dark caves enclosed the opposite side of the valley. I felt I was in a secret place, an Irish Brigadoon. The silence rang in my ears. In the quiet, not a soul was to be seen in that landscape outside of time.

After a while Joan joined me, and, slowly, we hiked the length of the valley in silence. We dodged fresh sheep droppings and saw tufts of wool hanging on branches of hawthorn, but no sheep. I wanted to press on and find the sheep that could survive in this inhospitable landscape. Oddly, there were none in the valley below. We climbed higher and higher, into the wind, until we pulled ourselves up on a peak of rough rock that allowed us to see across the broad valley beyond. All along the horizon, gray limestone lay luminescent under the silver light filtering through the clouds. The wind had grown fierce, so strong that as I leaned into it, it supported my body against the pull of gravity.

Joan and I sat in our own islands of silence, surrounded by the roar of the wind, surveying the seemingly infinite sweep of rock that ran out to greet the horizon. It was good to take a rest, both to catch my breath and to absorb the vastness of the scene. I tried to imagine the struggle to scratch a living from the rocky land below. I thought I had worked hard over the past two years, piecing together a new life for myself in the North Carolina mountains, but my work was easy compared with the back-breaking, bone-grinding, never-ending work the Irish must undergo here just to provide the fundamentals of food, clothing and shelter. The wind, which I found so invigorating on that afternoon, would be hostile as a permanent adversary. I wondered what it was that kept people in such a harsh environment; then I thought of how wedded we are to the land where we are born. From birth we are taught the ways of survival on our native land and with our native people. I thought of the basic skills and knowledge of nature required of the people to thrive on this island of limestone in the sea, skills and knowledge which I, with my university education, completely lacked.

When Joan and I finally stood up to go, I saw something move out of the corner of my eye. There in the distance were sheep, blending into the rocky landscape, nuzzling nosefirst into the rock crevices for shoots of grass and wildflowers. No shepherd, just rock and sheep free to forage—and howling wind pushing the gray clouds across the sky.

In the next days, Joan and I traveled up the west coast, following roads where the land met the sea. Our little car persevered over the narrowest of single-lane roads up into County Mayo, which Joan declared the most beautiful county in Ireland. We arrived midday at the home of Michael Joe and Alice, a retired couple related to Joan. We found them snug and sheltered from the wind in their small home on "the Hill" in Corraun, a community of a few houses overlooking the incredibly beautiful Clew Bay. Alice had a hot meal ready for us when we arrived. We ate in the kitchen around a slow-burning peat fire, peat that she and Michael Joe had cut from the land and dried a few weeks before.

After lunch, Michael Joe took me out back and showed me the remains of the original stone croft where he had been born and raised along with his seven brothers and sisters. It was a rectangular one-room cottage built by the family, originally with a thatched roof. He used the building as a work shed in which he kept the tools and paraphernalia he needed to maintain his sheep and do his fishing. He took me to the local dock and showed me a haul of giant crabs and sea urchins that, as I watched, he cleaned out with a sharp knife and set on his stone wall to dry. He pointed to a solitary tower standing on the opposite shore of Achill Island. "It was the strong-hold of Grace O'Malley," he said. "She was a pirate who sailed the waters of the west coast pillaging towns and vessels, bringing her booty back to the tower for safekeeping."

That afternoon, when everyone else elected to sit by the fire and

watch the soccer match between England and Ireland on TV, I
chose to take a walk on the stretch of beach not far from the dock
where Michael Joe's currach, a small round fishing boat, bobbed in
the waves. Of course there was wind. It was a rare, brilliant day of
sun, showing off the deep colors of the Irish coast at its best. Across
the cobalt-blue waters of Clew Bay I could see the mountain
Croagh Patrick crowned with its halo of clouds.

I sat on the edge of a high dune and watched the myriad facets
of sunlight sparkling on the water. I tried to collect my thoughts. It
was difficult to center down; my body had been in motion so much
of the time, and my senses assaulted, though pleasantly, with so
many new experiences, and now that infernal wind roared in my
ears, coming at me from behind. What I need is a quiet place out of
the wind, I thought. I moved forward and stepped down under the
grassy ridge of the dune onto the warm sand. By sliding down a
little further, I discovered that the wind shot over my head, pro-
viding me with a haven of warmth and stillness on the leeward side
of the shore. I lay back and relaxed, watching singular clouds
change shape as they moved by overhead. In the clouds I saw my
life parading across the sky: first a child, then a wife-mother, then a
woman walking on her own.

If too many men, I said to myself, spend their lives fighting battles for turf and dominion over rival clans, too many women spend
their lives defining themselves in relation to others. In my case, I
lived my childhood in my passion for music. I played the piano four
hours a day and spent my spare time outdoors, exploring my town
and the fields and woods beyond. Looking back, that's what I
remember. Then I burst out of my first family into the world,
defining myself as musician and adventurer. When I married, I
slipped into the family I would help create and became wife and
mother for thirty years. But I could feel a shift even as I made my

wedding vow. When the veil was lifted, I felt I had lost my liberty. My attempt to maintain my individual freedom within family life became a daily struggle. Like so many wives and mothers before me, I gradually sacrificed my own will for what I thought was the good of the family. I knew something was wrong, but I couldn't grasp how to right it.

To give my life meaning, I defined myself as both heart and anchor of my family. It was inconceivable to me then, that we—husband, wife, son, daughter—could break apart. But after many years, the inconceivable happened, not once, but twice. In the black of a winter night, the phone woke my husband and me from sleep. It was a stranger calling to tell us our son was dead. He had been lying on a sofa watching the eleven o'clock news with a friend, when his heart, inexplicably, stopped beating. Peter was just twenty-two, standing tall and handsome on the crest of his man-hood, and now a doctor I didn't know was saying my son did not exist. Never, never, have I felt so helpless, so useless. And, oh, I had not been there to comfort him in his dying as I had been present to hold him in my arms at his birth.

For a long time I was drawn into the darkness of that black night. My body grew so exhausted from the strain of the loss that I felt I was a hundred years old. Every minute I was afraid my daughter would die, and I lost all desire to live myself. Then grad-ually, but also rather quickly, the rest of the family I had worked so hard to build fell apart. The cord that once had bound my husband and me to each other grew taut, then snapped. Our daughter, stunned and confused, went her own, tentative way.

Abruptly I found myself living alone in a little white house with a porch, overlooking a long, grassy lawn and the Smoky Mountains beyond. My moments of peace came when I drank my tea each afternoon on the porch, pouring it from a china teapot my mother had given me just before she died. I sat out on that porch in all kinds of weather, taking the necessary and long-overdue moments for myself in contemplation of where I had been, and gathering strength to move on.

The solitary and hypnotic clouds passing by overhead had become a bank of gray mist. Turning my head, I saw a yellow wildflower bobbing in the wind. It made me think of Joseph Campbell, who once held up a daisy and, with a broad smile, asked, "Meaning? People want life to have meaning? Does this flower ask, 'What is the meaning of my life?' No! It just blooms. It just is!"

And that's the way I saw my life. Just being; no questions asked.

When we bid thanks and farewell to Michael Joe and Alice the following morning, I could hear Joan getting directions for the seaweed baths. "Just what we need to relax," Joan said. It was to be our final day in the west of Ireland. We headed inland through Mayo and over to County Sligo on yet another windy day. We found Kilcullen's Bath House on a slice of the most enticing Atlantic beach we had seen on the trip.

We wasted no time in entering the mid-nineteenth-century establishment, and within minutes, we each found ourselves in a private room equipped with a long, claw-footed enamel bathtub and a wooden box in the corner, hissing steam. The tub was filled with warm seawater and a mound of seaweed; the Turkish bath had a round hole so that my head was free to breathe the cool air, while the rest of my body sat sweating in the steaming wood box. The routine was to begin in the box, then lounge in the bath, and, finally, stand up and pull the cord to release a shower of ice-cold seawater—then begin the whole process again. There was no time limit. We could repeat the routine as often as we liked and stay as long as we wanted.

It is hard to describe the feeling I had lying in that warm tub of seaweed with the wind howling outside the window. The oils from the boiled seaweed coated my body in a rich, satin smoothness I had never felt before. The seaweed itself was downright sensual. I lay back and floated easily in the warm saltwater. This was all I needed to be happy. And no one was knocking on the door telling me it was time to go. When I tried to sit up, my hair was so drenched with the heavy oil that I could barely pull myself upright. Each round of steam, bath and shower was more pleasureful than the last, until my body had relaxed to the point of weightlessness. All it took was pure physical pleasure and no deadline to put me in a state of quiet bliss.

Finally I toweled myself dry, dressed and joined Joan in the bright solarium for tea and cakes. I was in such a trance when we departed that I left my favorite sweater hanging on the chair in the sun.

Ireland is a small island, and by the next evening, I was on a ferry named *Felicity,* being blown by the West Wind across the Irish Sea to Wales.

When my Welsh friends Wil and Rosemary Rees greeted me at the Fishguard dock, they were all smiles. For me, Wil and Rosemary are the quintessential Welsh couple: both handsome with gray hair and blue eyes, their open manner revealing their lust for life. Wil, the perennial teacher, had planned a tour for me on the way home, and he wasted no time directing Rosemary to drive us to the site of the best-preserved dolmen in Wales. Pentre Ifan, meaning "Ivan's Homestead High on a Hill," is the remains of a megalithic burial site. It has been standing for some five thousand years in a wind-blown field not far from Crymych. Sheep grazed lazily around the striking structure of great, standing stones, one huge stone resting like a tabletop on the other three.

It is impossible to stand before these ancient monuments without slowing down. It is a staggering and humbling thought to imagine your ancestral peoples walking these fields thousands of years ago. All that remains of their presence are these standing stones, the skeletal gateway to an aboveground burial chamber once filled with ashes that have long since disappeared. I couldn't help but wonder what would remain of my life. Ashes that would return to the earth? Memories that would vanish with the wind?

We headed back home to Laugharne, which is nestled in a valley, out of the West Wind, on the south coast of Wales. This seaside town, famous for its Norman castle and the Boat House, which served as the last home of Dylan Thomas, is so much like home to me that each time I leave it, I feel as if I am ripping my own roots out of the soil. I first came to Laugharne when I was twenty with my sister Marnie. Traveling as students, with one Pan Am bag between us, we sought out this medieval town to see for ourselves where the legendary Welsh poet had lived. Then we convinced our mother, who had passed on to her daughters her love of Thomas's poetry, to visit this town and the land of her ancestors after her divorce.

One summer I lived in Laugharne with Wil and Rosemary in their bungalow overlooking the fabled town. Now I had returned to be with them again, attracted by the simple way of life in the town that lives side by side with the rhythm of the tidal river Taf. Over a span of six hours, the waters of the Celtic Sea and Carmarthen Bay pour into the riverbed of the Taf, flooding its banks; then in the next six hours the waters recede, flowing back out to sea. This whole miracle is accomplished by the moon, that sphere of silver light, that muse, which rises and sets to the music of its own rhythm, over both river and town.

I spent my days in Laugharne walking Sir John's Hill, climbing the ruins of Laugharne Castle and happily eating Rosemary's sponges—lightly baked cakes—with my afternoon tea. I drank Buckleys at the Brown's Hotel, where Dylan Thomas used to drink and play cards with his friends. And one evening the three of us, joined by friends, ate a savory Laugharne meal of cockles from the river, laver bread made from local seaweed, and soup made with nettles from the fields nearby. After we finished the dessert of Wil's fresh fruit salad, we watched the high tide overflowing the green banks. The estuary had swollen to cover the entire valley and looked more like a lake than a river. Rosemary turned to me and asked if I would like to walk across the river to the other side. "We could do it tomorrow," she said, "at low tide." She consulted her tide table, and we made a date to leave the house at one o'clock in the afternoon.

The next day at the appointed hour Rosemary and I headed out to cross the river Taf, walking down the steep driveway, down Gosport Street and across the Grist Square. We walked the cinder path below the castle and continued on the red rocks that serve as foundation for the Boat House and the old Ferry House next door. Because of the strength of its tidal currents, no one swims in the Taf. As a child, Rosemary had seen her best friend, age ten, suckèd into the current off the jetty where they were swimming and drown. She has deep respect for the power of the river.

We slipped out of our sandals and began walking, barefoot, over the damp sand and mounds of seaweed drying in the sun. It was low tide, and what had been under water in the early morning was now sandy river bottom exposed to the sun. The wind picked up as we walked along the shore next to the deepest channel of the river, which always contained fresh water flowing down from the river's source in the hills. Rosemary led me out onto a plateau of warm sand that we walked over until we came to the river's shallowest point. There, we crossed warm fresh water, feeling the tug of the current on our legs. We walked across slippery black mud, and Rosemary told me its story: the "slime" is a mixture of river mud and of coal dust from the freighters that used to come up the river to deliver coal. The local people, or the Larnies, as Rosemary called them, would gather the slime in baskets, mold it into balls and let it dry briefly, before poking a hole through the balls with a stick. Slime balls were excellent slow-burning fuel for the home fires. They would glow hot all night long and still have enough fire left for the women to start cooking breakfast when they woke on cold mornings.

As we walked on, I gathered cockle and mussel and razor clam shells. We walked past the Scar, a point thrusting out into the river where it made a turn to the left around the base of Sir John's Hill. Rosemary said the Scar was always covered with seaweed and still looked the same as it did when she was a child. Air bubbles on the surface of the sand signaled cockle beds; we stopped to look and then walked on to a line of fishermen's stakes standing upright in the sand. Across the river channel was the Ginst, a windy stretch of strand where thousands of rabbits inhabited the grassy dunes, yet another place where Rosemary ran as a child. We stood and surveyed the riverbed, marveling at how broad it actually was. We looked across to the medieval town and saw it from a completely different perspective. Then, noting the placement of the sun, Rose said we had better turn back so that we would have plenty of time to cross the river before the tide came in.

We turned around and walked back, this time closer along the river channel. My feet felt on holiday to have had such a long hike free of shoes. Finally we reached the crossing point, and legs tired, we fell into the warm water, letting it wash over us, clothes and all. We couldn't help laughing; it felt so much like being children again. Rose told me she hadn't taken this walk in years, and that it was bringing back all sorts of memories for her.

We sat in our spots in the rushing water, sinking into the sandy bottom as the force of the wind and water pushed against our backs. While Rose became lost in a reverie of her childhood, I felt the feminine force of the river, powerful enough to quench fire, yet flowing softly, firmly, around me. I could easily identify with the flowing motion, always moving on, yet definable in its own right. I thought of the Irish river Liffey carrying the woman's name, Anna Livia Plurabelle, in James Joyce's fiction.

In a time when it was not always popular to praise the feminine, I could say I loved being a woman. I thought of coming into my own, belatedly, but nonetheless vibrantly: of not feeling shy about being myself and doing what I desired to do. I thought of the sheer thrill of composing my own music, performing and recording it. "Windblown Watkins," the reviewer said of the photo on the cover of my first solo album. That photo was taken on a beach much like the sands by the river Taf.

I considered the women I have known in my life. I thought of Gail, who used to say, "I have to get out of the house. I can't stand being alone with my thoughts." In contrast, I have liked the company of my own thoughts. I recalled Myrtle, who stood gallantly by her handsome husband, herself a brave warrior against the cancer that lived in his body for decades—and when she was finally alone, she summoned the strength to begin life anew on her own.

I thought of Les, who was struggling with the nightmare of Parkinson's disease. "I have to dance with it, or I'll go mad," she told me. "I am dying." "We are all dying," I said. And that made me think of Renate, so beautiful, talented, sensitive, kind. Some of the deepest conversations I have ever had with a woman were with her. But Renate had been dying of leukemia in Germany while I was innocently writing her encouraging letters from North Carolina.

When I received the black-bordered card in the mail announcing her death, I couldn't believe it. I hadn't even had the chance to say good-bye, to wish her farewell, to tell her I loved her.

I was sinking deep into the sandy river bottom. The water was rising, approaching my neck. I looked over at Rosemary and saw her laboring to stand up. I pulled my heavy body upright out of the rushing stream. We shook ourselves off, like dogs after a cool bath, and laughed at the sight we would make walking back through town. We returned to the red rocks and dry seaweed beneath the Boat House. As we sat down to clean our feet and put our sandals back on, I heard the sound of waves forming in the river channel. It was the tide coming in.

"We're just in time," Rosemary said. The salt water from the sea was meeting the fresh water from the hills and trying to overpower it. Of course it was succeeding, and each minute it progressed a little farther up the channel. We stood a while and watched. The wind and the sun began the chore of drying our clothes. When we reached home, we turned and looked back across the town and down the hill toward the river. The broad sands we had just walked were once again covered with wild, rushing water from the sea.

That evening, my last in Wales, I walked alone by the river in the light of the slow-setting sun. I looked out across the estuary and could see that the tide had turned once again. It was flowing back out to sea. I could hear the cries of the water birds punctuating the steady drone of the wind. Nature's music, I thought, and I remembered the "singing fence" on the Isle of Skye from a previous trip I had taken to Scotland. It was a fence of metal pipes at the edge of a cliff high above the sea, and when the wild wind blew through the pipes, it produced a music as haunting as the pipes of Pan. For a moment my heart leaped, knowing that on this journey to my ancestral land, my body—like that magical fence—had become an instrument of the wind.

• • •

I have never flown east from Europe before. I feel a sense of intrigue, soaring above alien territory. The world of the East I am entering seems exotic compared to the familiar West I am leaving behind.

I am flying over Pakistan now, toward India. The sky outside my plane window is black—no stars to get my bearings, just the low hum of the jet engines and the sure knowledge that I am riding the wind. I feel the cold on the other side of the plastic pane. High above the earth, enclosed in silver metal, I am surrounded by blackness. The void beyond is too immense to contemplate. I grow tired, but sleep, like a fickle lover, evades me.

Nepal
Beyond Words

Things that are real are given and received
in silence.

—Meher Baba, "Love Me Silently"

Royal Nepal Airlines Flight 206 alights with the grace of a bird on the runway of Tribhuvan International Airport in Kathmandu. The long flight from Zurich and the restless night in New Delhi's antiquated airport have left my body bone-weary, yet my spirit is keen for new adventure. I step onto the red-brown earth of this ancient crossroads of Asia, feeling a kinship with those who have walked here before me.

Within minutes I am standing with my luggage on a platform outside the small airport terminal, looking for Jay Pal (pronounced Jay Paul), one of my former international students, who promised to be here to pick me up. Instead, I find a crowd of a hundred men, holding handmade signs, shouting in a babbling confusion of half-a-dozen languages, hawking their hotels, tours and rides to the city. A small man with shrewd, appraising eyes approaches, circles me, and attempts to woo me with his offerings. No Jay Pal.

I wait twenty minutes, and when the men begin to depart in the smoky haze of late afternoon, I find a phone. I have to dial several times on a black instrument, reminiscent of the phones I used as a girl, before connecting to a startled woman's voice. It's Jay Pal's mother, who calls him to the phone. "Oh, Nan, are you here?" he asks in surprise. "I'll be there in fifteen minutes."

Half an hour later I am sitting in the left front passenger seat of Jay's jeep, riding with him through the airport gate into the city of Kathmandu. The first thing that catches my eye is a man—not a boy—peeing in the dirt by the side of the road, playing with his little fountain by making a high yellow arc in the air. How different from the buttoned-up bourgeois citizens of Zurich I was among just yesterday. An eight-hour flight east has delivered me from the First World to the Third World, from one of the richest cities on earth to one of the poorest.

I am not comfortable with the terms "First World" and "Third World" because they rank nations by level of material wealth and industrialization, assuming that to be an industrialized nation is to be "developed" and "first," while to be a traditional rural culture is to be "undeveloped" and "third." These are reductive terms created and used by the Western establishment to describe the cultures of the world in superficial, materialistic terms, devaluing other aspects of life. For me, life is far richer and more complex than that.

Over the years, the people I've known from Asia, Africa and native cultures in the United States have given me glimpses into their ways of life, cultures that are still deeply rooted in the natural and spiritual worlds, which for them are inseparable. In the West, we have been uprooted from our original affinity with nature—our Judeo-Christian creation story states that we were banished from the Garden of Eden. As a result we no longer live in harmony with the natural world, but see the planet and its abundant diversity of life as ours to use and "develop" for our own gain. Many cultures do not measure life by gross national product and economic wealth, however. The Himalayan kingdom of Bhutan measures its success by an indicator called gross national happiness! It is this great divergence in values—materialism versus spirituality, literacy versus orality, private ownership versus common property—that is at the root of so much tension in the world, tension that I can't help but observe as I move from an industrial to a rural culture.

Pushing his jeep through the choked traffic of town, Jay is laughing and upbeat. I've known him for many years through his undergraduate and graduate studies in the United States, and here in Kathmandu he makes me feel as if I've come home to visit one of my own children. Even on this cloudy afternoon, the bright colors of the women walking gracefully in their saris refresh my tired eyes. Jay Pal circles monuments, crosses bridges, and then, finally, turns down a dirt road in Thapathali, an area in the south of town. "There's my mom," Jay says, and I see her, petite and beautiful, standing in the dust next to a metal gate. Indira Shrestha greets me with the traditional "Namaste" (pronounced NahmaSTAY), folding her hands in prayer position and slightly bowing her head. I repeat the same gesture and Nepali word, derived from the Sanskrit, meaning "I salute all divine qualities within you."

Stepping over the threshold, I clunk my head against the metal bar at the top of the entrance gate and am immediately brought back to earth. My head hurts, and I take it as a reminder to slow down. Inside the walled grounds, the public chaos of traffic is left behind, and I enter a private, peaceful garden filled with red poinsettia trees and flowering plants. I step into the warm brick house, removing my shoes at the entrance, and walk in my stockinged feet on elegant carpets I can't help admiring. "They were handwoven in my uncle's carpet factory," Jay says. I am offered a cup of herbal tea, which I gladly accept, and am shown to a comfortable bedroom upstairs. I'm given a key to my room and told to keep my door locked.

Though I have not slept for twenty-four hours, I am too excited to sleep now. I find a cloth in the neighboring bathroom and clean the cut on my head. I unpack my two dresses and hang them in the cupboard. I explore my room, examining the pictures and keepsakes of Jay's younger sister, who has left Nepal and lives "faraway," as her mother says, in the United States. I look out the window at the sky and know that though I am in a foreign country on the other side of the earth, the sun, moon and stars are still there as my familiars.

Gradually the bed entices me. I stretch out on the colorful quilt and close my eyes, but my body still feels in motion, as if it's being carried through the air. With nearly twelve hours' difference in time between my bedroom back home and this bedroom in Kathmandu, night has become day, and my body has not adjusted to the change.

My mind is active and slides easily back in memory to sixteen years ago when two Nepalese students—the first from their country—arrived at Western Carolina University. My husband and I, founding members of the university's host family association for international students, invited the students from Nepal to our house for dinner. Our two children, both in high school at the time, were curious and shy about our guests-to-be. We consulted our atlas and located the country in the Himalaya tucked between two giant neighbors, China and India. We learned Nepal was roughly the size and shape of North Carolina, and we could relate to that.

When Himank and Somendra, two good-looking, athletic young men with beautiful brown skin and black hair, stepped into our house, we all smiled with relief that there was no language barrier. Their English was excellent, for they had been educated in British boarding schools in Nepal and India. We sat down to a meal of meatballs and rice, and the new students were pleasantly polite. To break the formal silence, we began asking them questions. One of us asked, "In Nepal, do you eat with a knife and fork or with chopsticks?" Somendra answered easily, "My people eat with their hands." We tried to imagine what that meant. We learned that their chief diet was lentils and rice and that they never ate beef because cows, the givers of milk, were considered sacred in their Hindu religion. My daughter, a vegetarian by nature, heartily approved, while I felt embarrassed I had served them meatballs. When asked to give a simple description of life in Nepal, one of them said, "It is two hundred years behind the United States." Again, we tried to imagine what that meant. Then my husband asked what the students wanted to do with their lives. Himank said he wanted to become an engineer to help solve the technological problems of development in Nepal. Somendra said simply, "I want to become prime minister." My son's eyes popped. We knew then that these two young men were extraordinary people.

That dinner table conversation was the beginning of my intense involvement with the people of Nepal. Our family became the host family for Himank and Somendra for four years, and for their brothers and cousins and friends when they came to the United States as students. We eventually hosted more than twenty students from Nepal, India, Bhutan and Sri Lanka.

One Christmas holiday, when both Peter and Ellen were home from college, our Nepalese students brought a visitor to our house on New Year's Eve. Dr. David, an American-educated Lebanese who chose as a young man to make his home in Nepal, had come to the United States to recruit the first team of Friendship Force to go to Nepal—Friendship Force is a cultural exchange between peoples founded by former president and first lady Jimmy and Rosalynn Carter. Because of my family's involvement with Nepalese students, my husband and I were asked to apply to be members of the team.

As the darkness of that New Year's Eve intensified, I lit more candles around the room, and it seemed a corresponding fire began to burn inside of me. I was smitten by the idea of journeying to Nepal. I had never thought it possible before—Nepal was, after all, on the other side of the world—but now I was being invited to be a guest there. I could barely contain my excitement and promised Dr. David when he left that I would apply for the Friendship Force team.

In the sunlight of the following day, however, I learned my husband, though he was as fond of the Nepalese students as I was, did not share my desire to travel to Nepal. Other commitments prevented him from going, he told me, assuming, therefore, that the matter was closed. But the fire kindled in my heart on that New Year's Eve continued to burn, and for the first time in my marriage, I determined I would take a trip overseas without my husband, reversing the twenty-five-year history of his six overseas trips without me.

Ten months later I was on a plane headed west across the Pacific, a member of the first Friendship Force team to Nepal. After that brief introduction to one of the most charismatic countries on the planet, I vowed I would return.

I awaken early to sounds of motorbike and truck traffic coming through my open window, reminding me I'm in the city. I hear a knock on my bedroom door and open it to find Jay Ram (pronounced Jay Rom), a young boy of about nine, smiling and holding a tray carrying a pot of hot tea. In Nepal the day begins with Ilam tea, grown in the mountains of eastern Nepal near Darjeeling, India's famous teagarden district.

When I join the family downstairs for breakfast, I find Jay's mother slowly sipping her tea. Indira does not share her son's preference for a Western breakfast, but will eat her hot meal of lentils, vegetables and rice later in the morning. I join Jay eating Indian corn flakes with hot milk and a piece of toast browned in a small toaster with metal sides that open out. It reminds me of the one my grandmother used to have.

I glance into the kitchen and see Jay Ram squatting on the floor over some old newspapers. He is crouched on his haunches scaling a fish on an ancient-looking hand-wrought metal implement, which he holds steady with his right bare foot while running the side of the fish across the vertical blade. The fish scales are falling onto the newspaper on the floor. Devi, a girl of perhaps twelve, brings me a fried egg, which she has cooked on a two-burner hot plate. These two young people are children whom Indira has agreed to take from poor circumstances and educate, giving them a home in exchange for their domestic service. They attend the local school, and she sees to it that they learn their lessons. They do not eat with us at the table.

Indira is one of the more remarkable women of Nepal, and I feel fortunate to know her. Widowed in her early thirties, she was left to raise her three children alone, since Nepalese custom prevents widows from remarrying. Shortly after her husband's sudden death, she had the shrine in the garden built to honor his memory, and she tends it daily with offerings of marigolds and other fresh flowers. It is here where she says her *puja,* or prayers, each morning. In her student years Indira studied music and science and received a master's degree in biology, an extraordinary achievement for a Nepalese woman. As an adult, she harnessed her strong will by entering public service and formed the Women's and Children's Development Foundation to improve women's literacy, which she says is one of the most pressing problems for Nepalese women.

"Hurry, we must see the king!" Indira suddenly calls to anyone within hearing. It seems everyone knows that the king is leaving his palace today to fly to London for a medical checkup. That means crowds will already be on the main route to the airport, the same road I arrived on yesterday. I join the little band of people leaving the house, and we walk a few hundred yards down to Airport Road. Throngs of people of every description are lining both sides of the broad street, with policemen holding everyone a discreet distance back. Indira passes me a handful of pastel fluff, a cross between confetti and popcorn, along with marigold petals, which are considered auspicious. She tells me, in her limited English, to throw them when the king's motorcade drives by.

I look at the crowds lining the street, Nepalese people of many different ethnic groups, all ages and far more poor than rich. I am standing behind a group of men wearing traditional Nepalese jackets and *topis* (Nepalese caps). They are busily talking in Nepali and I imagine they are discussing politics, for the king and royal family along with the shaky National Parliament are constant topics of conversation. Suddenly a wave of cheers runs through the crowd, passing from right to left. Peeking between the heads of the men in front of me I can just make out, in the black limousine speeding by, the stiff profile of King Birendra, sitting in the back seat behind a closed window, staring straight ahead.

I let my handful of confetti and marigold petals fly, and they land on the shoulders and caps of the men before me. This is the first king I have ever seen, and I am disappointed at how remote from his people he seems. I wonder how he and his queen, dressed in the finest fabrics, riding in an expensive car, can rest at night when they know that many of their subjects suffer some of the worst poverty in the world. These people lining the streets must feel like Cinderella, having missed the ball.

Walking back to the house, Jay Pal asks me if I would like to join him on a drive to Patan, one of the three original city states in the Kathmandu Valley and one of the oldest Buddhist cities in the world. Without hesitation I agree, and within minutes we are driving across the Bagmati, the main river traversing the valley. "We call the town 'Lalitpur,' which means 'City of Beauty,'" Jay says. "Today it holds the richest trove of architecture in the valley."

Around 250 B.C., Ashoka, the Indian emperor whose mission was to spread Buddhism throughout his empire, had four Buddhist *stupas*, or shrines, erected at the four corners of Patan, and they are still visible today. In the center of the city is the Durbar (palace) Square, which features the royal palace and many temples of various styles. The square's main buildings were built by the Malla kings, who reigned over four centuries in the valley.

What strikes the visitor first is that the temples are made not of stone, but of handmade brick and wood. What gives the temples their distinctive character is the pagoda shape: tiers of gradually smaller wooden roofs held up by ornately carved supports. Thirteenth-century architect Arniko, one of the Newar people inhabiting the valley, was the first to design pagoda roofs, which allowed the smoke from the temple's sacrificial fires to escape. Arniko was so famous for his design and craftsmanship in the Kathmandu Valley that he was invited to serve the Ming emperor in China, where his pagoda design soon flourished. The road leading from Kathmandu to the Tibetan border today is named the Arniko Highway in his honor.

What I like most about wandering amidst these sacred buildings from centuries past is seeing how they are still in use today and very much a part of the daily scene. Barefoot and sandaled men crouch on their haunches on the brick steps of the temples. They talk and observe the stream of people walking through the square from the nearby market, the tourists like me coming to see this beautiful place and the pilgrims who visit the temples to make offerings and pray. Happily, motorized traffic is kept from the center of the square so that the people, the elaborately decorated bicycle rickshas, the sacred cows, a few monkeys and the pigeons have the place to themselves. In the late morning sunlight Jay and I enjoy watching the people watch us.

The aroma of grilled meat and vegetables drifts our way, and following our noses, Jay and I walk into a doorway behind a temple that leads into a long dark space. Inside, people are sitting, talking and eating, while the cook keeps up a steady conversation with them. The tables are full, so we sit down on rough wooden benches and lean up against the cool brick wall. Jay asks in Nepali for a plate of marinated raw buffalo meat with rice flakes. I pass on the raw buffalo and choose *bara,* lentil pancakes that arrive piping hot from the stone grill. No utensils are served, so we wait a moment for the food to cool and eat it with our hands, washing it down with a bottle of Fanta.

We stroll back out into Durbar Square, admiring the noonday sun on the golden statue of a once mighty Malla king, perched high on a column in front of his palace. A pigeon struts on the king's head, while a finely wrought cobra rises behind him, its hood protecting the king from harm.

The office is bright with white walls, hardwood floors and bamboo furniture. Jay Pal is sitting at his desk, checking for e-mail messages on his computer. He gives me a printout of a few lines from my daughter, Ellen, and my heart skips a beat—she is so far away, yet this little scrap of paper is a tangible reminder of her presence.

I am visiting the modern office of the Canadian development team for whom Jay Pal works, funding environmental projects. He says it is a small operation with limited money for projects like water harvesting and reforestation, but he is glad to be doing something positive to improve the deteriorating environment of his beloved Nepal. His favorite part of the job is taking field trips into the rural areas, where he rides donkeys into the villages and works with the local people, helping them learn better ways to cultivate their land.

Climbing back into Jay Pal's jeep, we head north across town. The road gets narrower and rougher as we leave the city behind. We drive past settlements of Newars, who are known for their exquisite woodcarving. Jay, whose family is Newar, says you can spot Newari dwellings because the people live communally in attached houses made of the local brick. We are in a rural scene now, with chickens fluttering as we pass and shepherds herding their sheep along the roadside, while stray cows saunter lazily down the center of the lane.

Jay is taking me to one of the many sacred places in Kathmandu Valley. As he drives he reminds me of the importance of knowing something about Hinduism in order to understand Nepalese culture. A country comprising some thirty distinct tribal cultures, Nepal is the last Hindu kingdom in the world. Hinduism, which began in India more than four thousand years ago, can be baffling to an out-sider, with its plethora of gods and goddesses, so to simplify things, I think of the various divinities as representing many aspects of the one spiritual force, which is a palpable presence throughout the land.

Learning about the Hindu gods is a little like learning about the ancient Greek gods: they all have their own attributes and powers, and the people love to repeat their stories, which have come down through the ages in numerous epics, religious writings, and works of art. The main trinity of Hindu gods represents three basic func-tions: creation, preservation and destruction. Brahma is the creator, Vishnu is the preserver, and Shiva is the destroyer. The three gods have many incarnations, or aspects, and they have wives and consorts and vehicles on which they ride. The most beloved god in Nepal is Shiva, and many of the temples are devoted to his worship.

Jay Pal drives through narrow streets dotted with bare-bottomed children, pecking chickens, sleeping mangy dogs, and people walking and bicycling amidst the sporadic vehicular traffic. Everywhere people are carrying burdens—women walk from the well with metal water jugs resting on their hips, women and men walk, bent over, in small groups of three or four, carrying large bundles of cut firewood on their backs. The people are barefoot or in thongs on the dirt streets—few people wear leather shoes in this land of the sacred cow.

We reach the village of Budhanilkantha and the pilgrimage site: the reclining Vishnu. The king, considered an incarnation of Vishnu, the preserver, is forbidden to gaze upon this sacred image of the god, lest he die. We enter the holy shrine along a small stone path and then walk down a few steps. Lying before me is a large horizontal statue carved around the sixth century from a sixteen-foot-long slab of black stone. The statue is generously covered with marigolds and vermilion powder, the soft reds and golds paying brilliant homage to the hard, black stone. Some of the wilted flowers have fallen into the pond surrounding the statue and are floating in the cloudy water.

This is the great god Vishnu in one of his incarnations, Narayan, floating upon a bed in the cosmic ocean called Nara. Hinduism teaches that a lotus grew out of the primordial Narayan's navel, and from the lotus came Brahma, who created the world. The myth seems akin to the opening of the Judeo-Christian creation story, found in Genesis, where "darkness was upon the face of the deep. And the Spirit of God moved upon the face of the waters." In both traditions, the primeval ocean is the source of all creation.

The serenely sleeping Vishnu as Narayan rests on a bed made of the coils of Ananta, a huge snake whose eleven hoods rise up and circle the god's head in protection. In Narayan's four hands are the four symbols of Vishnu: a chakra representing the mind, a mace for primeval knowledge, a conch shell for the four elements, and a lotus seed for the moving universe.

Each morning at nine o'clock a priest descends into this basin and washes the face of Narayan. He, along with the pilgrims gathered, places flowers as offering while attendants ring bells. Once a year great numbers of pilgrims, who stay in *dharmasalas*, or rest houses, celebrate the Festival of Budhanilkantha.

The religion in which I was raised is different on the surface from my host family's Hinduism. Quakerism is sometimes called the mystical branch of Christianity. Quaker meetinghouses, unlike the elaborately carved Hindu temples, are as plain as they can be with beige walls, no altar, no stained glass windows, just benches facing in the same direction except for the facing bench at the front, which looks out over the others. My meetinghouse in Pennsylvania, where I grew up, was built in 1793, but the meeting minutes begin in 1683, when Neshamina Monthly Meeting was established, just one year after William Penn, the English Quaker who founded Pennsylvania, arrived in the American colony on the sailing ship *Welcome*.

Unlike Hinduism with its hierarchy of gods and goddesses, and unlike other branches of Christianity with their many rituals, Quakerism is stripped of all sacraments and has but one ritual— that of silence. George Fox, the founder, and other early Quakers like William Penn, rebelling against the intolerance and patriarchal rule of the seventeenth-century Church of England, wanted to return to the simplicity of the fundamental teachings of Jesus. The focus was on the two great commandments: "Love the Lord your God with all your heart, with all your soul, with all your mind," and

"Love your neighbor as yourself." Quakers today still strive to do just that. Without any ordained clergy, each Quaker—man and woman alike—seeks to put into practice the ideals of equal respect for all people, tolerance for the many different ways of life, and peaceful settlement of disputes. From childhood, I have felt at home with the Quaker way of life and worship.

I gaze at the reclining Vishnu and watch the colorful but quiet commotion of the pilgrims entering the shrine. In silence, they come to pray. This is the marvel of Nepal: the blending of time-honored spiritual practices with the everyday toil of life. Hindus and Buddhists, young and old, come to this ancient shrine for a moment of peaceful veneration in their busy lives. This spirit of reverence must be at the core of what sustains these people's diffi-cult and laborious lives.

It is evening and we three—mother, son and foreign visitor—have come together around the dining table to share a meal. Young Devi, who tries her few words of English on me, says "Good evening" and brings in steaming bowls of freshly cooked cabbage, cauli-flower, greens, curried lentils boiled down to a consistency of sauce, and steamed white rice, along with a plate of cut-up fried fish—the same fish I saw Jay Ram scaling on the floor in the morning. Every-thing is bite-size, so there is no need for a knife at the table. Little is spoken as we serve ourselves; then Indira gestures to me to take a fork from the little stand of utensils on the table. I decline and join mother and son, eating the Nepalese way, with my hand.

Indira and Jay begin mixing the food on their plates together with their right hands—only the right hand is used when eating, for the left hand is reserved for unclean chores. They push a vegetable into a little mound of rice, knead it together so that the curry sauce penetrates the rice and vegetable, and then, turning the four fingers of their right hands into mini shovels, scoop up a small amount of the mixture and put it into their mouths, using the thumb to push the food off their fingers. When I first try this, it feels cumbersome and sloppy; rice grains and sauce fall into my lap. But after I get the hang of it, it feels good. It is a sensual experience, eating with your hand—feeling the warm sauces on your fingertips, the different textures of the food.

With our dinner we are served glasses of water, and I hesitate to drink it, thinking it has come right from the tap. The Nepalese, however, have developed daily routines to ensure they have safe drinking water. They boil their water for twenty minutes; then those who can afford to, filter the boiled water through a simple charcoal system. After the water has been purified, it is stored in clean thermoses and served at the table. The water is kept covered to protect it from contamination by malarial mosquitoes and other insects.

I look around the dinner table at my hosts enjoying the meal without a lot of talk, and I think how far I've come in these eighteen days of my journey. I feel comfortable here in Nepal and relate to the people easily, despite our differences. I don't know which I enjoy more—discovering what I have in common with these graceful people or learning to appreciate the differences in our ways of living.

Coming together in silence with my Nepalese friends is a deeply unifying experience. Silence can be a powerful tool for communing with others on a deeper level. By silence, I mean a profound time without words, without language, for the sounds of the world are always about us.

I think of the people I watched earlier in the day, bringing their offerings of marigold petals to the sleeping god Narayan. The act of giving an offering was enough; there was no need to speak.

Taking time each day to retreat from the spoken word brings us in touch with the natural world and with the universal spirit. Perhaps I am able to live so easily among these people on the other side of the world because we are communicating at a level beyond our surface differences. I am with people whose greeting and farewell refer to the divine qualities within each of us. It is in that divine spirit beyond words, beyond language, that we have much to share.

Pulchowki
Flower Mountain

> Heaven descends and Earth flies up
> to meet on a mountain peak:
> they embrace and kiss with red lips of pleasure.
> —Lakshmiprasad Devkota, "Prayer on a Clear
> Morning in the Month of Magh"

Indira watches me at breakfast and looks on disapprovingly. She says she has lived in Kathmandu all her life and has never trekked up any mountain. She tries to discourage me from taking this day trip with her son Jay Pal, saying it will be too much for me, that as a woman I should not climb the mountain, especially not as an older woman.

Pulchowki is the highest peak in the green mountains that surround the Kathmandu Valley. At 9,050 feet, the height of many of the snow-covered Alps, it is taller by far than anything in the Great Smoky Mountains where I live. Yet, here in this temperate climate, Pulchowki is covered with green trees and flowering shrubs, and, in fact, its name means Flower Mountain. I am eager to leave the city, to get some exercise and to climb this legendary peak.

Trekking Pulchowki is a favorite hike for Jay Pal, and I'm pleased that he is willing to take me with him. On a rough and rocky path barely wide enough for the jeep, we drive a short distance beyond the base of the mountain, and then Jay pulls the jeep off the path into the bushes, hoping it will not be found. Carrying my day pack, I set out on foot in the cool morning air for the four-thousand-foot climb.

I like to hike, but I am admittedly best on gentle inclines like the ones in the countryside around my home. I decide that if I am to reach the summit of Flower Mountain, I must choose the tortoise's sure, even pace, and I fall easily into a good rhythm that feels right. Jay chooses the pace of the hare, and now and then when there are shortcuts through the rhododendron and bamboo, he ascends a slippery mud path and waits at the top for me to come around the horseshoe bend in the rough road. I try two of these steep mud paths, but much prefer the even pace of the gradual ascent to sliding backwards in mud, grabbing at branches to keep from falling.

Two different paces: youth and age. I mention my thought to Jay as we walk up a long incline together. He laughs and encourages me to keep up the steady rhythm. It was my idea to join him on this climb, and he has doubts about whether I can make it to the top. After hearing his mother's discouraging remarks at breakfast, I understand why. He is used to bringing "the guys" on this hike with him and says even his young girlfriend does not want to make the climb.

We continue talking about the differences between youth and age, and Jay tells me he likes the way the ancient Hindus formulated the course of a human life into four distinct stages: the first, childhood and youth; the second, the householder years building a family; the third, retirement to a forest hut to live simply and talk philosophy (Jay says wives went with their husbands in this stage); and the final stage, renunciation of the material world in preparation for death.

When I hear this, I say that I am certainly past the first two stages. I feel as if I lived them both to the fullest, putting a lot of energy into whatever I was doing at the time. The first twenty-three years of my life were childhood and youth, years of preparation. Then came thirty years of the householder stage in marriage, twenty of which were spent raising two children. I am clearly in the third stage now, living quietly in the country, where I have simplified my life and enjoy looking at the bigger picture in a philosophical way.

I am once again focusing on my own life, as I did in my youth, trying to manifest what I studied and prepared for in my early years. I am presently in a time of bearing fruit, but in a different way from bearing and raising children. I'm using my talents and bringing them to fruition: performing my own music, translating German literature, writing about subjects that interest me, like my travels. I even have tangible products to show for these efforts—several cassettes of music, a new CD and publications. These are things I did not do when I was married and raising a family. I enjoy this creatively productive stage with free time for contemplation.

When my active years are over, I hope I will be able to surrender the material world willingly before I die. Thomas à Kempis, the fourteenth-century Christian monk, wrote in *Imitation of Christ* that he prayed he would not have a sudden death, but rather would be given the knowledge that he was dying so that he could prepare himself for losing the earthly body and returning to the divine spirit. I hope I have the courage to do the same.

I think of the seventy-seven-year-old woman I saw at Jay's big family gathering a few days ago. She had just reenacted the *pasni* ceremony, achieving seventy-seven years, seven months, seven days of life, the precise moment, according to Hindu tradition, when a person enters the revered state of old age. It was a repetition of the earlier pasni first-rice-feeding ceremony performed when she was a seven-month-old child. It is remarkable for this woman to have achieved the milestone of seventy-seven years, when the average life expectancy for a woman in Nepal is fifty-three.

A woman sitting next to me at the family gathering leaned over and spoke to me softly, "We think of her as nearly a saint now." When I heard this, I contemplated how different this is from my own culture, which worships youth instead of age. Sonam, one of my international students from Bhutan, once told me that his people did not put their aged relatives in old-age homes. "We take good care of them at home," he said. "We bring them tea in bed."

The revered older woman at the party sat serenely, her legs folded under the silk of her sari, a quiet look of resignation and acceptance on her knowing face. She did not take part in the activities of the other women. She did not sit on the floor helping to peel a mound of grapefruits and section them into heaping bowls. She did not work in the kitchen cooking the rice and fish, the chicken and vegetables. She sat on raised cushions and received her glass of juice with a nodding slight smile, her eyes gazing off into the distance, the singsong music of the younger Newari women's chatter forming a soundscape for her reverie.

I was glad to see the older woman honored, for in this culture women perform much of the hard physical labor. Yesterday at Jay's house I was surprised to find Indira, instead of Devi, cooking the dinner of *kwanti*, a hearty multibean soup. When I asked why, Indira explained that Devi was menstruating and was given four days of rest. At first, I thought this was a way of honoring the natural rhythms of a woman's life, but later I learned a woman is considered to be unclean during her period, when her body is cleansing itself. She is not permitted to handle food at this time.

The glimpses I have had of the role of women in this culture are contradictory. At that same family gathering a few days earlier, we crowded around a large table to eat tender bits of chicken and fish and an array of vegetables, served family style in generously filled bowls. I was seated to the right of the host, the eldest brother of the clan. When I remarked to him that he had a wonderful big family, he told me he had made a family tree and asked if I would like to see it.

After dinner the eldest brother brought out a large white scroll, about five feet square, and unrolled it on the floor over a bright red handwoven carpet. The India ink drawing was in the shape of a large tree, and it told the story of the family for seven generations. Each man was represented by a branch, with the eldest forefather being the trunk of the tree. When a man had several wives—polygamy was not uncommon in the past—there were offshoots of the main branch for the various sons by the different wives. If a man had no children, he was represented by a broken branch. What stood out for me was that the women were represented by leaves, not branches. When a girl was born, she was given a leaf with her name on it, but the family tree did not record her marriage and children. Indira, for example, was represented by a leaf, but her son, Jay Pal, was not on the tree because he came through a maternal line. It was a totally patriarchal tree.

As Jay and I climb ever higher on Pulchowki, I feel the difference in the quality of the air. Jay estimates we are at roughly seventy-five hundred feet, and besides feeling cleaner, the air feels lighter with a cool, green taste to it. My lungs, irritated from the polluted city air trapped in the valley below, appreciate the change. We are walking through a forest thick with forty- and fifty-foot-tall rhododendrons. They must be an incredible sight when their profuse red and white blooms burst forth in the spring. No wonder they call this Flower Mountain!

It is quiet here. An occasional bird call rings through the trees. I stop a few minutes for a water break and look up to the clouds ahead. Though the sun is shining brightly in the valley below, clouds surround the peak of Pulchowki, and I wonder if I'll be able to see the famous views from the summit.

I think about the craze for trekking in Nepal that has occurred in recent years. When the first wave of foreign mountain climbers returned to the West in the 1950s to tell their tales of conquering Himalayan peaks, part of their story was about the hike in to the base of the mountains they were going to climb. These accounts inspired other adventurers to go to Nepal, not for the climbing but for the hiking. The word "trekking" was popularized in the 1960s to describe those hiking trips in Nepal.

Approaching nine thousand feet, the air becomes distinctly thinner and moist. The crown of clouds continues to rest on the peak of Flower Mountain, and the weather has changed to a cool rain. Jay suggests that we turn back, it is just more of the same, he says, but I have come this far and want to reach the summit. I continue walking steadily up the path. We are in a cloud forest now, one of the last dense forests, almost constantly under clouds, that survives in central Nepal.

Reaching the top of the mountain, we pass a telecommunications tower and two white buildings of a small army camp. Two soldiers watch as we walk by. The summit of 9,050 feet is up a narrow footpath of steep flagstone steps. My knees, begging for a rest, struggle to hoist my weight up these last steps of the way.

Finally out on the summit, I take a very deep breath. I feel jubilant to have come this far and this high, a record for me. I am thankful to have the good health and energy to do this. It doesn't matter that the view is obscured by clouds. I sit down on a large stone and give my legs a respite from the three-hour-and-forty-minute climb. I eat a sweet tangerine with Nepalese crackers and drink *pani* (water) from my bottle.

I like the mystery of the summit enshrouded in gray veils of clouds far removed from the daily business of the valley below. I love the stillness of the place. I love breathing the thin air, which refreshes my spirit as well as my body. I want to stay here and listen to the silence of clouds swirling slowly around the peak, the muted drip of water on stone, the whisper of prayer flags blowing gently in the breeze. There is a peacefulness here that beckons me to stay.

A stunningly good-looking young couple emerges over the top step. The beautiful girl, wearing a flowing deep brown *punjabi* tunic over stylish slacks with black sandals displaying elegant bare feet, walks straight to the small Buddhist shrine and, circling clockwise, takes a bit of vermilion powder from each of the four sides of the shrine, placing it on her forehead. She is receiving blessings from the Buddha. Then quietly, with eyes lowered, she walks to the bell mounted in a wooden frame on stone. She pulls the rope to its clapper and the sound rings out into the thin air. The tolling reverberates from the summit, much like the ripples from a pebble cast into a pond. It is a simple gesture, tolling the bell and listening to the tones vanish, yet in this deeply spiritual culture, the dying sound signifies the impermanence of life.

I watch the young couple standing together in the stillness, gazing into the clouds. Silence returns, filling my heart with praise.

The Bagmati
Dream of the River

> The Great Work now, as we move into a new
> millennium, is to carry out the transition from a
> period of human devastation of the Earth to a
> period when humans would be present to the
> planet in a mutually beneficial manner.
> —Thomas Berry, *The Great Work*

As I settle back in the garden swing to enjoy the morning sunlight flickering across the poinsettia blooms, Jay Ram brings me a glass of hot tea. The young boy then sits down on the ground near my swing and, smiling happily to himself, begins to trim the stacks of greens and long white radishes that have just been picked from the vegetable garden.

When Jay Pal joins me, I compliment his mother's walled garden, saying that it is a refuge of beauty and repose in the midst of hectic city life. I am surprised, then, to learn that when Jay's parents built the house in 1974, it stood alone in the country surrounded by rice paddies. What had once been a grand view of the mountains is now blocked by three- and four-story apartment houses, whose walls stand adjacent to the garden wall. The city of Kathmandu, like cities everywhere, has swelled in the last decades in an attempt to accommodate its population explosion.

I ask Jay to take me on a walk through his neighborhood of Thapathali, and he gladly agrees. We step through the metal gate, leaving the peace of the garden behind, and immediately join the stream of commerce on the dusty road. As motorbikes whiz by and trucks rumble to negotiate a curve, men stand outside a motorbike repair shop talking, and women walk along the side of the road, bearing loads of straw on their heads, ignoring the honking traffic.

We walk single-file around corners and down fenced lanes until we come to an elementary school, once the family home of Jay's parents. Jay greets the watchman at the gate in Nepali, and he permits us to enter. The dirt school yard is neat and orderly, filled with small fruit trees planted in rows. The soprano voices of young children can be heard coming from the many open-door classrooms. We step inside one of them and see a dim space crammed with navy-blue-uniformed pupils, whose dark brown eyes look up from their desks as we enter. The teacher bows her head in greeting and smiles at us as the children turn back to their work, copying out letters in little notebooks. Although Nepalese law requires five years of education, from ages six to eleven, few children actually complete the schooling. There is a severe lack of trained teachers and learning materials, and after the first grade, the student drop-out rate is huge. These children look cheerful, however, and the school vibrates with their energy. When we move back out into the dirt courtyard, we pass a colorful but reeking outhouse that serves as toilet for the several hundred pupils.

Continuing our walk through the neighborhood, we head toward the Bagmati and as we approach, trash in the streets becomes increasingly obvious. Finally we come to an open space that looks, at first glance, like a city dump. Malnourished cattle forage among trash heaps, stray pink and blue plastic bags blow about in the light breeze, insects hover in the air. As we approach the river, the stench is so great that I cover my nose and mouth with my scarf. In the distance a large island of garbage floats in a stream that seems to have no current. The water is a stagnant brown-black sludge, barely moving. We walk closer and find the bloated, decaying carcass of a cow stretched out on the riverbank, its head in the water and rump heaped on the bank. Insects swarm over the rotting flesh. It is hard to believe that this is the holy Bagmati River, which flows south into the holiest of holy rivers, the Ganges. This is where Jay used to swim as a boy.

"You could get sick from just breathing the air here," Jay remarks, as we continue to gaze over the barren wasteland. I am shocked at what I am seeing and ask Jay how this place of misery came to be. I learn that the once healthy riverbed used to stretch across the open space that now looks like a city dump. The horrific change is due partly to indiscriminate dredging for sand needed to make cement for the brick housing boom in Kathmandu. When the dredging continued too deep and too close to the foundation of the main bridge crossing the Bagmati, the bridge collapsed. With no money to rebuild it, the Nepalese went for years without a replacement. Finally the Japanese invested some of their foreign aid in the project, but instead of training Nepalese workers, the Japanese sent in their own bridge-building teams. The Nepalese got a bridge, but not the know-how to maintain it, much less to build other bridges.

I see the new bridge several hundred yards away and how the course of the once healthy river has been diverted. This is the sad side of Nepal, the environmental devastation that the tourist guidebooks are only now beginning to mention. My 1987 Insight Guide, *Nepal*, speaks of the Kathmandu Valley: "Think of the capital as a marvel of a microcosm, a flawless emerald in a filigree setting."

A ray of hope flickers. I say, "But Jay, you could use your American degrees in environmental science to educate your people and make a positive change for your country. You could lead your people to recover a healthy environment and restore the natural beauty of your land." Jay looks at me and shakes his head slowly. "The people of Nepal have a different priority, Nan. They want one good meal a day and a place of shelter. I would be the laughingstock of Kathmandu if I tried to make cleaning up the environment a top priority." I am bothered by Jay's sense of futility, but I know he is doing the most he feels he can in his village projects with the Canadian development team.

I take another look at the Bagmati in her misery and think of her sister rivers around the world that also suffer from pollution. Surely these rivers must be dreaming of their sparkling pasts, their once beautiful courses through valleys. Thomas Berry, the visionary theologian and ecologist and author of the Sierra Club book *The Dream of the Earth,* warns us that an anthropocentric view of life jeopardizes both mankind and the planet. As I look at this ruined river in Nepal, I think of the children I just saw in the local school. They will not have the opportunity to enjoy this river as a swimming hole the way Jay Pal did just twenty years ago.

Traveling the earth, I see easily the cumulative effects of humankind's behavior. The human race once lived largely in harmony with the natural world, and mankind's impact on the earth was minimal. But as our population grows exponentially and increasingly fewer people understand the crucial balance necessary to maintain a healthy planet, we approach a point of no return. We have inherited the results of our forebears' actions, and we in turn are leaving the legacy of our lifestyles to future generations. I yearn for people everywhere to come to their senses and live in ways that benefit rather than destroy the earth.

We walk back home through the streets of Jay's neighborhood lost in thought. When I visited Nepal in 1987, the South Asian Association for Regional Cooperation happened to be meeting in Kathmandu. The heads of state of the seven member countries were present. The Royal Nepalese government and army had taken heroic measures to clean up the city for the distinguished visitors. I remember the streets were well swept, the state buildings and religious temples and shrines freshly painted. Old wrecks of vehicles and heaps of trash had been hauled off the streets, and the tattered ricksha drivers banished. I stood in the crowds along the downtown streets as Rajiv Gandhi, prime minister of India, was whisked past in a black limousine. The air was cleaner then, and the Bagmati River was not yet ruined.

The first time I saw poverty and degradation up close, I was a young girl, about eight, accompanying my father on a Saturday afternoon to the tenements of inner Philadelphia. My father was a Quaker and a dentist, and he combined those two interests on his free summer Saturdays by volunteering to give dental care to children whose families couldn't afford dental services. We would drive twenty-five miles into Philadelphia and bring the children back to our home in Langhorne. When their dental work was finished, the kids would join our family for meals and play in the back yard before we would return them to their homes in the city. Sometimes they would stay overnight if their dental work was particularly complicated. My father liked to take one of his three daughters along on each trip because he thought it would put the child coming for dental care at ease to be with another child, and because he thought his daughters might learn a thing or two by seeing how others live.

I remember one particularly hot Saturday when I rode with my father to the city, where he first checked in with the Friends Neighborhood Guild. There he obtained the name and address of a family whose child we would take home for the day. He and I then walked to the address and up a flight of long wooden steps, where we met the mother of a large family living in a crowded, dirty tenement. I asked to use the bathroom while my father was talking to the mother and I was directed down a dingy, narrow hallway to a small room with a door that hung crookedly on its hinges. In it were a bathtub and basin caked in brown grime. The room smelled of urine, and when I looked in the toilet I saw a bloated dead rat floating in brown water. I fled the room in fright.

The shock of that visit is still with me today. I was a suburban girl glimpsing urban poverty for the first time. My father knew exactly what he was doing by taking me along with him: he was opening my eyes to the inequities in the world. When he brought those boys and girls home to fix their teeth, he was doing a lot more than fixing teeth. He was bringing two disparate worlds together in the hope that they would learn something from each other. I think he was trying to teach me the fundamentals of compassion and understanding in a society filled with inequality. My father had an eagle eye for injustice and was never shy about taking action, whether it meant joining the school board to improve the educational system or helping a black family buy a house in the all-white planned community of Levittown, Bucks County, Pennsylvania.

Those Saturday trips with my father as a girl were followed in my teenage years by weekend work camps in the poorest sections of Philadelphia, also organized by the Quakers. I remember going, full of hope, into my first house with a gallon of white paint and a big brush and finding knee-deep trash on the floor of the kitchen. Empty cans of Spam and Campbell's soup lay amidst banana peels, paper and garbage. The young law student who was my partner and I tried gamely to convince the overweight woman lying on a sagging metal bed in the next room to help us clean her kitchen, but she just lay there moaning indistinct complaints mixed with insults. I wondered if the roles were reversed, if I would do the same.

During that experience I began to question whether an outsider, no matter how well-intentioned, should attempt to show another person how to improve her life, if that person has not requested the outsider's help. This, I think, is a question we must ask ourselves at all levels of society. Real change, real learning occurs only when a person requests help. When outsiders tamper in any way with the affairs of another culture, the balance within that culture is disturbed. When Sir Edmund Hillary, with the best of intentions, sponsored schools for the Sherpa communities in Nepal, the children were taught to read and write by non-Sherpas in a non-native language (the Sherpas have no written language). One of the effects of that schooling has been a gradual disintegration of the local Sherpa culture.

Throughout history, enlightened souls have shown us in their words and actions how to live in harmony with our fellow humans and with all life on earth. Iris Murdoch, the British philosopher and novelist, said it well in one of her essays: "Love is the imaginative recognition of, that is respect for, the otherness of another person." Respect for the otherness—a beautiful and necessary aspect of love, of understanding and relating to all kinds of people. One of my childhood heroes, Albert Schweitzer, took this thought one step further. He taught "reverence for life," extending respect beyond humankind to include all forms of life.

But I am thinking today about Nepal. Even the Nepalese admit that their country and people need to make massive changes to avert environmental collapse, so why is the situation only getting worse? In one of the most naturally beautiful regions of the world, why has just about everything gone wrong?

My mind leaps to the neighboring Buddhist kingdom of Bhutan, where the king, often criticized in the Western press for his undemocratic ways, runs his country with a firm hand, yet with compassion for his land and his people. He has taken strong measures to limit foreign influence, strictly controlling both the amount and quality of foreign investment and tourism. An enlightened dictatorship, one might say. In taking this position, he is preserving the traditional culture, dress, language and religion of Bhutan and improving the lives of his people without plundering the land. This purposeful approach seems to make more sense than the laissez-faire one I witness here in Nepal.

In the twentieth century, people all over the world stood by and watched the degradation of their home, the planet, while in pursuit of a better life. This is a grand paradox, for there is no better life on a ravaged planet. It is as if we have forgotten that our health is inextricably linked to the health of all life on earth.

Each of us can learn from seeing a beautiful river ruined. The Bagmati serves as a wake-up call to become responsible citizens of our own place on earth, to summon our courage, energy and vision to make the dreams of the earth come true.

Kathmandu
Music as Prayer

Music is the art of arts and the science of all
sciences; and it contains the fountain of all
knowledge within itself.
—Hazrat Inayat Khan, *The Mysticism of Sound*

When I ask Indira what she has been doing with her
music, she proudly shows me a new cassette of
songs in Nepali, some of which she has written
herself. I am impressed—a picture of her lovely, still youthful face
graces the cover—and though I can't read any of the accompanying
Nepali, I am eager to hear her music. Like me, Indira revived her
interest in music after her children were grown, and she is now
active in a music school here in Kathmandu. It seems odd to call this
genteel woman a singer-songwriter, but that is one of the many
aspects of her full life.

Indira plays the cassette for me, and I am particularly touched by
the title song, which she translates as "Without You." In it she sings
of longing for her departed husband and of her solitary life without
him. Her clear soprano voice betrays a sadness that seems to be at
the root of her being. She tells me that in a few days she will record
a classical Indian song at the radio station to be broadcast over
Radio Nepal. When I ask if I may accompany her to the recording
session, she cocks her head quizzically to the side and then agrees.
Seeing my interest in her music, she invites me to attend her

morning practice session with her tabla player, in preparation for her appearance on the radio.

"You cannot have music without tabala," Indira tells me, adding an extra syllable to the word. She is speaking of a set of Indian hand drums. Both Indira and I are fascinated with the structure of music, with the harmony and forms that are the framework of songs and instrumental compositions. On a small Yamaha keyboard I show her the circle of fifths and the seven modes that define the harmony in Western music. Then it is Indira's turn to show me the ten *thats* (pronounced tots), or basic scales, used in North Indian classical music, which is what is performed in Nepal. I write the ten thats down, one by one as I learn them, on the lined music composition paper I have brought with me, and I sing them each with Indira. I am most fascinated with the scales that sound exotic and different from the Western scales I have been playing since I was a child. With the basic thats as fundamentals, Indira tells me how she sings her ragas, or classical Indian songs. She accompanies herself on a simple four-stringed instrument called a tambura, which is tuned to have a drone effect, anchoring her improvisations in the chosen scale.

Now, in the morning coolness, I greet Indira's tabla player, who teaches at the Music Institute and performs in four-star hotels in town. We enter a small outbuilding designated as the music room and sit down cross-legged on a handwoven carpet on the floor. Indira carefully unwraps one of her tamburas, a small one, and tunes it to an electronic tuner powered by a battery—the old world meets the new. Hearing the notes she has chosen, the drummer uses his tuning hammer to adjust the pitch of his tabla. The instruments that Indira and the drummer play have been used for centuries, and except for the stronger modern metal of steel, they are still made today in much the same way as they have been for hundreds of years.

Indira begins to stroke the four strings of her tambura, then slowly she starts to sing, improvising her melody within the limits of her chosen scale. She sings freely without strict rhythm, beginning to tell the story of her song. After she has laid the foundation, the tabla player enters, a necessary partner in her song. He establishes a rhythm that is far more complex than classical European rhythms, using different strokes on his hand drums to vary the accent and beats of his playing. I listen carefully, trying to follow the rhythm and melody, though I can't understand the words being sung. Sitting on the carpet-covered floor of this little music room together with these two musicians, I hear Indira's clear, sweet voice sing of longing for a distant time of love.

After a good hour of practice, we reenter the courtyard garden, and the tabla player bows with the same gesture of "Namaste" as when he arrived. Indira's niece approaches with a plate of fresh red flowers as offering for the morning prayers at her uncle's shrine. Indira turns to me, and putting her thumb into the bowl of vermilion powder and flowers, she marks the center of my forehead between my eyes, leaving a *tika*, or bright red mark of blessing, which I wear proudly for the rest of the day.

I believe my love of silence, learned in Quaker meetings as a child, informed my passion for music. It all began with the big, dark upright piano my parents kept in the upstairs hall of our house. I have been told that as soon as I could reach the keys, I started sounding out the notes to make melodies I had heard, and by the time I was three I was playing tunes on the piano. My father's dental office was downstairs in the front of our house, and among his patients were nuns from a nearby convent. When the nuns came for their appointments, they heard my playing upstairs and told my father that I had a special talent and should be given music lessons. One nun in particular, Sister Lucretia, who I thought was beautiful in her austere black habit, continued to cajole my father until he enrolled me, at the age of four, with a local piano teacher who was director of music at a private institution for the mentally retarded. I was her first "normal" pupil.

I learned to read a staff of music before I learned to read words. I remember the oversized staves and large, round, black notes balanced precariously on lines and spaces that were defined by elegant clef signs. I worked hard to learn the physical coordination required to push down a particular note with the proper finger at the proper time, but my teacher's frustration must have been even greater than my own, for when my four-year-old fingers did not do my bidding, she whacked them with a ruler. Even as a young child I grasped the paradox of my joy playing the piano intuitively by ear at home versus the anxiety of trying to play "correctly" for my finger-whacking teacher.

Later, I studied with a wonderful young woman, who was sensitive to my latent abilities and who brought out the best in my playing. I had perfect pitch and enjoyed spinning irreverent improvisations, including musical sketches of my teachers for the amusement of my classmates. In my study of music I learned discipline, physical technique, focus, desire for perfection. Over the years with many fine teachers, several of whom were faculty members at Curtis Institute in Philadelphia and performers in their own right, I learned the basics of the classical piano repertoire. I performed regionally in solo recitals, in concert halls and in piano competitions, and I won prizes, recognition and encouragement to make performance my career.

Often, though, my desire for perfection made me a nervous wreck. Like Gandhi ending a fast, I would take sips of orange juice as my only nourishment on the day of a performance or an important lesson. But when I was at home, I would play the Lester baby grand piano, which my parents had bought for me, with a passion that knew no bounds. My father would leave the door to his dental office open so that his patients could hear me play. My youngest sister, Susan, would lie on the floor beneath the piano, listening and loving the loud parts best, and later became my official page turner when I played for school productions. My mother exhibited a forbearance I doubt I could equal if I had had a child who so dominated the living room with long hours of piano practice. Only my sister Marnie, ever alert to the humor and ironies of life, dared mock my fierce dedication to music. Once, when I was lost in the sound of music at the keyboard of the upstairs upright piano, Marnie crept noiselessly down the long, dark hall and then popped up with a shriek that rendered me witless.

In those young years, my central reference to life was through music. I was the pianist for my Quaker Meeting, accompanist for my school assemblies, and pianist and featured soloist for the school orchestra. Even on summer vacations, I sought out a piano to play, and I remember practicing in the back room of the tiny post office of a small town in the Poconos. To make the summer evenings fly while washing dishes, I taught my cousin Betsy a German duet whose words she gamely learned by rote; we never tired of singing robust versions of it together. Beginning when I was ten, I received annual season tickets to the children's and then the youth concerts of the Philadelphia Orchestra. When I watched Stravinsky conduct his own work, I thought he looked like a giant crane, long and lanky in his attempts to lead the orchestra. I was present at Toscanini's farewell concert in Carnegie Hall. During my senior summer I was a student at Tanglewood Music Center, where I reveled in being with fine musicians all day long, and I sang in a chorus with the

Boston Symphony Orchestra. When I sailed across the Atlantic on student ships, I spent hours in the ships' lounges, playing the piano. I would choose a theme, then spin a dozen variations, each in the style of a different composer. I remember an enraptured listener feeling tricked when I revealed that the variations I had been playing were based on the tune of "Three Blind Mice."

Now as an adult, after all of my training in classical music, my greatest joy is to create music of my own. That is why, in later years, I have been attracted to the organ and the synthesizer, both instruments that allow the composer to mix timbres of sound, as an artist mixes colors of paint. Musical sound is for me a creative tool, a language in which to express myself. Whether I am improvising at home for a group of friends, playing as organist in St. David's church or performing a concert in public, I would rather make my own music than play someone else's carefully rehearsed notes. I guess it's the freedom I like, the freedom to speak through music.

I arrive home alone at dusk to find the house in darkness. Indira tells me it is the night for "load shedding," the time when the electricity is deliberately shut off in this section of town for the two peak-use hours of the day. The government has taken this measure to ease the ever-increasing demand for electricity, rotating the load shedding around the city so that each district has its weekly turn. Even this does not solve the extreme strain on a shaky utility system, and it seems a strange expedient to an outsider, who knows that Nepal has extraordinary water resources that could be harnessed into more than enough hydroelectric power to satisfy the needs of its people.

Indira is in a desultory mood, casting about for something to do.

She asks if I would like to go with her to a benefit concert for the Women's and Children's Development Foundation—she doesn't like sitting in the dark house with flickering candles.

Outside in the moody dusk, Indira retrieves an old car from a garden shed and waits just long enough for me to jump in the front seat while Jay Ram swings open the metal gate. The car lurches out into the evening rush-hour traffic. I didn't know that Indira could drive—it's a rare sight to see a Nepalese woman behind a steering wheel—so I am surprised at this sudden turn of events.

Indira's driving style is totally different from her son's easygoing manner. Sitting low in the driver's seat, barely able to see over the steering wheel, she inches her way out into the steady traffic of the main road, honking the horn all the while. Slowly and gingerly we make our way toward the center of town, and Indira, gesturing with both hands, points out the stadium and the Martyrs Memorial beyond. We drive through the Old City Gate and past Freak Street amidst chaotic traffic, barely able to see in the dark night. Despite the precarious nature of the trip, I am not worried, sure that somehow we will arrive safely at our destination.

Gradually we come to streets so narrow that only one car can pass through at a time. Indira honks the horn as we thread our way through the lanes teeming with people until we turn into an unlit courtyard of old apartment houses. Here, near Kathmandu's Durbar Square, in the first private home built of cement in Nepal, Indira was born.

We walk back to the busy lane, through a doorway and into a festival of lights. A large high-ceilinged room is filled with people sitting on cushions and mats on the floor, with a few on folding chairs, all listening intently to a heated concert already in progress. People recognize Indira immediately; several men stand up from their chairs in the front row, and she and I are ushered to their seats.

I am sitting just to the left behind a shrine of Buddha with a replica of a temple on top. Each of the four sides of the statue is lined with smaller figures. The whole shrine is alight with oil lamps, ten on each side. These are tended by young girls using a vessel that looks like a metal teapot, from which they pour oil. Four large red candles in tall brass candlesticks are burning on each corner of the podium. Sticks of incense smolder a few feet from me, making the air heavy with sweet smoke.

The music is moving at a fever pitch. A lovely girl sits at the back of the small raised platform in the front of the room, stroking the four strings of the tambura. To her left sits a musician playing the sitar, the fingers of his left hand flying so fast up and down the long strings on the fretted neck that my eyes can barely follow them. The tabla player is to the right of the girl, playing exotic rhythms on his hand drums that seem to be in conversation with the rapid tones coming from the sitar. When the tabla and sitar players finish a long improvisational section precisely together, their eyes meet, their faces break into smiles, and then the music continues, each player becoming lost once again in the fusion of mesmerizing sounds.

When the music stops, there is hearty applause. A slender man walks to the side of the stage and, reading from notes, announces the next piece in Nepali. Then switching to formal English, I presume for me, the one foreigner in the crowd, he says the next raga is called "Raga Yaman" and is in F-sharp in the Kalyan scale. He explains that it is a classical song based upon the following words, which will not be sung:

We have come together four days.
Don't look at me hiding.

A singular thought—like the old Persian and Urdu verses I have read in translation, or like a Chinese haiku in its simplicity. The music begins, the oil lamps are filled and the smoke from the incense mingles in the air with the alluring melodies. My mind whirls from the intoxicating sounds of the tabla and sitar raised to glorious heights in music of passion and fire.

As the raga comes to an end, Indira takes me by the hand and leads me, through a throng of smiling faces, to a low door and a small narrow area with a long bench. She calls this "backstage." Soon the performers gather with us and seat themselves on cushions on the floor. More musicians join us, along with a distinguished elderly poet laureate, to whom I am introduced. There is much lively talk in Nepali and Newari. Indira is beaming, clearly in her element with the musicians and artists.

Soon young people begin handing out food. The plates are made from large green leaves of the *sal* tree that have been pressed together and stitched with slivers of straw. A savory mixture of *dal bhat takhari,* rice and curried lentils with vegetables, is served on the leaf plates, and we begin eating with our hands. A woman passes out tiny clay cups and a man follows, pouring what Indira calls "the local wine" into the cups. Eager to taste the homemade wine, I take a big swallow. The liquid is fire and heats my throat like the strongest whiskey. "Wine!" I exclaim, and everyone laughs, seeing my reaction to their local brew.

As more food and drink are consumed, the conversation level increases. A young woman who identifies herself as an English literature student at the university sits down beside me and tells me her favorite modern English writers are Alice Walker and Virginia Woolf. She says she is also a fifth-year sitar student of the performer we just saw, and we talk enthusiastically about Indian classical music. "It is like meditation," she says, and her teacher, who overhears, corrects her, saying, "No, it *is* meditation." I add, "It is a form of prayer," and he says, "Yes, exactly." I feel a close rapport with the musicians as we eat and drink and talk music together. We exchange cards, hoping that we will be able to hear each other play in other places, at other times.

After the food, there is a call from all the people assembled for the musicians to perform again. We return to the large room, the young sitar student sitting next to me. She leans close to tell me about the raga they will play. "It is a man singing about loving a beautiful girl," she whispers, "but the matchmaker has just fixed her up with another man. He sings of his sorrow of losing her."

The flames in the oil lamps flicker. The tambura announces the key of the raga and begins its sorrowful drone. The sitar delicately explores the sounds of the new raga until it is joined by the rhythmic beat of the tabla. The music swirls about the room, joining the incense smoke perfuming the air. Once again, sitting by my new young musician friend, I am borne away to the realm of the wondrous, of fire and heat, of clouds and rain, of meditation upon a story of a lover who longs for his beloved.

Kathmandu Valley
Innocence and Experience

> Take care with the end as you do with the beginning.
>
> —Lao Tzu, *Tao Te Ching*

Emerging from sleep on my first morning in the Thapas' house, I pull the curtain aside to see a terraced hillside of rice paddies outside my bedroom window. As if she knows I have just awakened, Shanthi knocks softly on my door and, handing me my morning tea, joins me in her robe. I first met Shanthi when she and her sister, Mona, came to North Carolina to visit their two sons who were studying there at my university. Shanthi's son, Bishwa, has made a life for himself in North Carolina, and Mona's son, Somendra, has established a business here in Lalitpur. It is good to see him again, now head of his own family, masterminding various business ventures and making sure that I am treated as an honored guest.

Shanthi's bright eyes show a merriment that betrays her love for life, and the two of us talk of our children and what has happened since we were last together. We share our hopes that our daughters will find opportunities for rewarding lives. Shanthi's youthful beauty belies the fact that she is a grandmother. She is at the center of her extended family, caring for her aging parents and enjoying the company of her grandchildren, who live nearby.

In time we dress, and with Mona, who lives in the house next door, we "three sisters" open the entrance gate to the family compound and turn south along the dirt road, the December morning sunlight slanting across our path. We pass children in navy uniforms walking to school with their schoolbags and water bottles, a woman guiding a little goat, and many women toting large sacks of raw wool, which they will spin into yarn at home. Mona, whose classical Nepalese features remind me of paintings I've seen of Hindu goddesses, nods her head briefly at a roadside shrine, murmuring a few words to herself; Shanthi greets a neighbor woman, and they pause for an animated conversation in Nepali.

Over a mile down the road, we turn west onto the property of Dr. David, the man who visited my home on New Year's Eve nearly twelve years before and who first invited me to Nepal. Here I find a carefully laid out estate planned by a visionary. An orchard of fruit trees and grapevines stretches the length of the lawn; poinsettia trees bloom in abundance. On terraces below, workers are constructing long greenhouses for the commercial production of flowers. A white Mediterranean-style house, reflecting the owner's Lebanese heritage, rests gracefully on the southern slope, catching the rays from the morning sun.

Dr. David, whose dark beard is now streaked with gray, includes us all in a welcoming embrace and leads us into the cool carpeted living area of his home, the white walls hung with striking oil paintings. He is attentive to all three of us and soon asks about my children. When I start to answer Dr. David's questions about Peter's death, tears suddenly course down my cheeks. I am surprised at this. Though I can speak easily about Peter's life, remembering things he did or said, the unexpected questions about his death trigger the release of sadness hidden deep within. Even after nine years, if I'm taken off guard, that sadness makes itself known.

We move to the aqua-tiled table in the sunny kitchen and enjoy a breakfast of eggs, cheese and fruit together. Sitting in the same kitchen as I did eleven years before, on my first visit to Nepal, I realize how I have changed since then. Peter's death has become the watershed of my life. Before he died, I lived in a world of innocence, each day striving, uninhibited, to achieve my dreams. But the death of my son marked my loss of innocence. William Blake spoke eloquently of that transition in his *Songs of Innocence and of Experience*, a book I have pulled off the shelf many times to read. I watch my host, Dr. David, who lost his young wife to cancer, and know that he, too, has crossed the bridge from innocence to experience. It has taken years for us to refocus and learn to embrace the sorrow of our loss within the joy of our lives.

If I were to name a single cultural site in Nepal that has thoroughly challenged my Western sensibility, it would be Pashupathinath, the venerable old temple complex on the banks of the Bagmati River, upstream from the pollution Jay Pal and I witnessed. Dedicated to Shiva, this is Nepal's most important Hindu temple and is a destination for pilgrims throughout the Indian subcontinent. In Somendra's household, Shiva is the patron god of Shradha, Somendra's wife, who fasts one day a week in obedience to her Hindu god, and who has given the names of Shivank and Shivani to her son and daughter in honor of her Lord Shiva.

The god who reminds us that out of destruction comes creation, Shiva is often represented with four arms and dancing in a circle of fire. In this temple, he is portrayed as Pashupathi, Lord of the Animals, one of his peaceful incarnations, so no animal sacrifices are made. A manifestation of Shiva's creative role, Pashupathi is shepherd to both animals and humans. The Nepalese believe that

Pashupathi offers them protection, so his name regularly appears in the king's periodic messages to the people, and it is to this temple that the king comes to seek the beneficent god's blessing before he sets out on an important journey. Pashupathinath (*nath* means temple) is a distillation of various aspects of the Hindu world that can be both fascinating and disturbing to a Westerner.

When I first enter the courtyard of the temple complex, it impresses me as being more like a town square than a sacred place. Runny-nosed children chase each other over the flagstones, and several boys squat on the ground playing a board game. Crowds of people come and go as assorted peddlers sell flowers, fruit and trinkets. What stands out for a Westerner is the statue of Shiva with his lingam, or erect phallus. I have read that inside the temple grounds, where I am not permitted to go, stone phalluses are worshiped and tended daily by Hindu priests. These phalluses are expressions of the procreative side of Shiva, and like the carvings of big-breasted goddesses or couples in erotic sexual positions found on temples throughout Nepal, they can be startling to a Westerner in their frank portrayal of sexuality.

I have come to this temple with Mona and Shanthi. They want to show me their local sights, just as I once played host to them in North Carolina. Mona and Shanthi are steering me now, giving me a push from behind, toward the temple entrance at the back of the courtyard where they know, as a non-Hindu, I am not permitted to go. They have a determined but amused look on their faces as they prod me forward, and I am not sure what they are up to. When I reach the temple entrance, I look through the gate and see the rear view of an immense brass statue of a bull raised on a podium to eye level. This, I am told, is Nandi, the god Shiva's vehicle or means of transportation, who represents fecundity. I hardly need to be told this, for the bigger-than-life brass bull, viewed from behind, displays large round haunches above huge brass balls that shine brightly in the afternoon sun—the last thing I would expect to find in a churchyard back home.

When I turn to look at my friends, they can hardly contain their delight. Having tasted American puritanism on their visit to the United States, they can't help but tease me, knowing that such vivid sexual symbolism would be a shock to my Western sense of decorum. Enjoying their mischievous sense of humor, I remain standing in the temple entrance, admiring the fecundity of Nandi, until a temple guardian spots me as an outsider and quickly shoos me away.

Mona and Shanthi lead me across a small footbridge over the Bagmati River. On the way, I smell roasting meat, and it makes me hungry. When I turn to look back across the bridge, I am shocked to see the cremation *ghats* (steps), and I realize I am breathing the smoke from burning human flesh. Covered in smoldering straw, the corpse of a man lies on the steps by the river, his legs and arms sticking out at the edges, as smoke from the cremation site rises eerily into the air. A man swathed in white cloth sits on his haunches, keeping watch over the body, adding pieces of straw and faggots of wood to the modest funeral pyre. Spires of smoke swirl and drift slowly into the air where we are standing, and then move on, following the course of the river. When the corpse has finished burning, Mona tells me, the ashes and remains will be swept into the sacred Bagmati River, and flow south into the Ganges.

In stark contrast to the dead on the steps of the temple is a lively scene of men and women bathing in the river. Shanthi tells me that women come here to purify themselves at the end of their menstrual period and that these people are performing ritual bathing. Nearby, I see *sadhus,* Hindu holy men who are wandering ascetics and seem to belong more to the spirit world than to this life on earth. One bearded sadhu with long braided hair, wearing colorful rags and walking barefoot, carries the trident of Shiva.

Not far from the funeral pyre, along the river bank, I see two people lying on pallets—an emaciated old man and an old woman. They have been brought here to die, and their feet are resting in the holy water of the river. In a few days, or perhaps hours, their bodies will be placed on the cremation pyre, just yards from where they lie dying now.

Though I am shaken by what I see, I realize that in a country with little modern medical technology, dying of illness or old age on the bank of a holy river—as people have for millennia—is natural and fitting. This Hindu way of dying seems more accepting of the natural process of relinquishing the physical body than the costly mechanical measures used in the United States to prolong life.

I think of my mother's death from breast cancer in the early 1970s. She was living alone after her divorce and, if she suspected she had cancer, she did not seek medical help, possibly fearing the disfiguration and the trauma of a radical mastectomy. When her strength had diminished noticeably, a friend took her to the doctor—my two sisters and I lived hundreds of miles away with our husbands and young children and did not know she was ill. There was little the doctor could do at the advanced stage of my mother's cancer.

Unlike the dying woman I see below at the river's edge, my mother spent her last days in the hospital where I was born, before the era of hospice, with her three daughters taking turns by her side. When I arrived, I learned that along with the routine nursing care, the medical staff was studying my mother's rapid physical decline by taking blood samples and tests several times a day. I became upset watching my frail mother in pain, so I told—not asked, but told—the lab technicians to stop taking needless tests. That modest action was the best I could do to give my mother a small measure of peace in her last days.

I realized then, for the first time, how private the act of dying is, how superfluous I felt in the presence of my dying mother. She knew she was close to death, and she did not struggle against it. She lay quietly in bed, forsaking her private reverie less and less to bestow her sweet smile on me.

The day my mother died, my sisters and I found a note to us in her purse. It ended with a quotation from the close of Thornton Wilder's *The Bridge of San Luis Rey*. "There is a land of the living and a land of the dead and the bridge is love, the only survival, the only meaning." My mother, who had been called a "master teacher" in her lifetime, was teaching even as she lay dying. She was leaving a signpost for her daughters, a reminder that through love, through the spirit, communication is always possible.

In the tableau at Pashupathinath on the banks of the holy river, I glimpse the rich tapestry of the ancient religion of Hinduism with its vast commingling of the earthly and the spiritual, the living and the dead. Visiting Pashupathinath has been an unsettling experience for me. It has challenged and confronted many of my assumptions about life, sexuality, spirituality, death. I am glad to have been brought here by understanding friends, natives who, when they know I've seen enough, take me by the arm and quietly usher me away.

Within walking distance of Pashupathinath is Bodhnath, one of the largest Buddhist stupas in the world, a holy destination for more than a thousand years, which serves as a center for the Tibetan community in Nepal. Entering the spacious compound where the huge dome-shaped shrine lies, I am immediately conscious of a cleanliness and order that is lacking on the streets of Kathmandu and even in the area around Pashupathinath. A woman is washing a small gutter where a trickle of water runs. The cobblestone street has been swept clean of dust. The many shops selling clothes, crafts and postcards are neat and organized. Buddhist monks of all ages in wine-colored robes move about the area, walking in a clockwise direction around the stupa, spinning the prayer wheels inscribed with the mantra, *Om Mani Padme Hum* (Hail! The Jewel in the Heart of the Lotus! Hum!) as they go.

I am visiting Bodhnath with Amrita, the young wife of Kanak, who was the most recent Nepalese student to study in North Carolina. She is expecting their first child. Together we walk clockwise around the base of the stupa, spinning the prayer wheels as the monks do. We ascend a small flight of steps lined with monks asking for offerings and begin to circle the bright white dome. We talk as we go, Amrita telling me how she is looking forward to the birth of her child, followed by the month of rest with her husband's family, where she and Kanak are living, and then another month of rest when she and her baby will live with her own family so that they can get to know their first grandchild. I am impressed how the young woman will be taught the skills of motherhood by both her own and her husband's mother within the child's first two months of life.

As Amrita and I stroll leisurely around the sunlit dome, I remember the birth of my son, Peter. My husband and I were living in a log cabin, hewn of whole logs by a Swedish craftsman, on a bank of the Fox River in Wisconsin. I was overflowing with joy, bringing my son to such a beautiful home on an August afternoon when the trees of the surrounding woods shaded us from the summer heat. In the following weeks, all the grandparents came to stay with us and meet their new grandchild, and my sister Marnie brought her son so that the young cousins could be together. Peter was a peaceful child and easily welcomed all in the family. I took advantage of the warm summer days and let him rest in the shade, naked on a blanket on the grass, the gentle breeze from the river caressing his soft skin. I was glad his eyes could learn to focus on the leaves of trees swaying overhead under the dome of sky.

Amrita and I continue to climb the several flights of steps and, reaching the top level of the stupa, we are greeted by a wonderful view of the surrounding neighborhood. Long strings of colorful prayer flags, originating from the top of the stupa's golden tower, are draped out to the edges of the dome below. The silk flags, inscribed with prayers, are transparent in the afternoon sun. The face of the Buddha, painted on all four sides of the tower, includes the third eye in the middle of the forehead, signifying the Buddha's ever-present clairvoyant wisdom, and what appears to be the nose, in the shape of a question mark without the dot, is the Sanskrit figure for number one, representing the oneness of life. I feel at ease in this Tibetan Buddhist community peopled by quiet, peace-loving monks.

Like Pashupathinath, Bodhnath is also a pilgrimage site. Both Hindus and Buddhists come here for meditation and prayer. Amrita, the daughter of a devout Hindu family, chooses to take her daily walk to this Buddhist shrine rather than to a Hindu temple. She, too, feels welcome and drawn to this tranquil yet thriving settlement.

The peaceful coexistence of religions in Nepal can serve as model for the rest of the world, for the country is a true religious melting pot. Here Hindus, Buddhists and devotees of ancient animistic cults coexist, along with a small number of Muslims and Christians, intermingling to such an extent that it is often difficult to distinguish between them. In the country's long history there has never been a religious war. I am agreeably surprised to learn that it is against the law in Nepal to proselytize or try to convert a person from one religion to another, and both parties—converter and converted—can be punished with a prison term.

I observe how beautiful Amrita looks in her royal blue tunic, her belly swelling with her impending motherhood, her face covered with a smile as serene as the painted face of the Buddha above her. I wonder what innocent dreams cross her mind as she joins me, contemplating the silk flags, whose prayers are being wafted heavenward on the soft wind of afternoon.

It is late afternoon, and Amrita watches as I pause at the base of the temple to pay the foreign visitor's price of admission. As we make the long climb up the steps to the ancient Buddhist holy site, Swayambhunath, I think of the endless variety of structures humankind has devised to create sacred space in which to worship. It is not a question of what is the right form of worship, but rather what kind of spirit is brought to the worship. It is always a challenge for me to center down, to leave behind the business of the day and enter into my own sacred space of the soul. Though I am not a member of the different religions I am witnessing on my journey around the world, I feel enriched, seeing the exuberance and diversity of expression in the churches and temples I visit.

When Amrita and I reach the summit of the hill on the western rim of Kathmandu Valley, we are rewarded with a broad vista of the sprawling settlements below. Legend says that it was on this high point that the patriarch Manjushri found the sacred lotus after the valley was drained of its ancient lake, and it was at the site of the lotus that Manjushri built his shrine. Swayambhunath is known today as the Monkey Temple because of the sacred monkeys roaming the grounds.

I step inside, walking past the large statue of the golden Buddha alight with hundreds of butter lamps, and in the dimly lit interior I can make out a row of Buddhist monks chanting prayers. Not all the monks are Tibetan and Nepalese; I see two white faces in the crowd, as intense in meditation as the others. I listen to the chanting and the mesmerizing drumming. Through the rhythmic drum beats and the recitation of prayers, the monks seek to raise their consciousness beyond the physical restrictions of the here and now to exalted realms of the spirit.

Returning to the open air Amrita and I wander separately through the immensely rich heritage of Buddhist and Hindu shrines intermingled throughout. The grounds of Swayambhunath embrace a collection of symbolic objects added to the sacred site through the centuries. I am attracted to the large *dorje*, or thunderbolt, a symbol of the absolute for Tantric Buddhists. I watch the monkeys scamper up walls and run to eat food set out as offerings.

Finally, tired and pensive, we walk slowly down the hill, down the long and curving stone steps from Swayambhunath. When we reach the base, an old Buddhist monk in a deep-red robe walks straight up to me with a pink flower. Placing the blossom in my hand, without speaking, he looks directly into my eyes with a radiant smile that permeates me; then silently he turns and is gone.

Pokhara
Annapurna

> Like the goddess Annapurna, she pulled out some parched rice from her bundle.
>
> —B. P. Koirala, "Madhestira"

I am staying with the family of Kanak, the last of my eight Nepalese students, in the Guheswari Heights section of Kathmandu. I enjoy immensely the high energy of this Brahmin household. Kanak's father is Nava Raj Subedi, the retired head of the single-party Rastiya Panchayat (National Parliament). This dynamic man rises each morning at five o'clock, takes a two-hour walk through the quiet streets of town, then returns home where he receives visitors—friends who come by to talk or old constituents who ask for his help in some personal or legal matter.

This morning there is a knock on my bedroom door at seven o'clock. Kanak, upbeat with a pleasant smile, cheerfully announces that a distinguished Nepalese professor of linguistics is here and would like to talk with me. I throw on my clothes and run down the stairs, passing the red footprints of the goddess Lakshmi on each step. These "footprints" of red flour paste lead from the front door of the house to the shrine of Lakshmi in the upstairs prayer room of Meena, Kanak's mother, who prays daily to the goddess for prosperity in her household. Meena, gentle and beautiful, is the senior woman of the family, and her young daughters-in-law, including

Amrita with whom I take daily walks, are expected to do whatever she assigns them in the household and to show her respect.

I find the professor relaxing in Nava Raj's sitting room and soon discover he is a scholar of Sanskrit, Hindi, Nepali, Latin, French and English. Dressed in a navy blue sweatsuit, walking shoes and an American baseball cap—he had studied many years before at the University of Wisconsin in Madison—he sips his morning tea as we talk about the Indian writers Vikram Singh and Salman Rushdie. His wife, dressed in a maroon sari, sits to the side and listens attentively as we talk. "I am an idealist, and my wife is a realist," the professor says, obviously relishing the subtlety between the two. "That can be hard," she replies with a smile.

Later that day I learn that the professor is known and loved throughout Nepal. Every school child uses his book as a language text, and he is a poet and translator of some renown. What he is most remembered for, though, is daring to denounce publicly the poetry, written under a pseudonym, by the former king. For such audacity, the then young man spent six months in jail until the king relented and released him.

I watch Nava Raj in the sitting room, conversing with his good friend, and I consider the lifetimes of energy these two men have devoted to their country, hoping to transform it into a modern state. But despite their efforts, their children continue to be enticed to better-run societies, where they choose to raise their own families. Himank, Nava Raj's eldest son and one of the first two Nepalese students my family hosted in North Carolina, has emigrated with his wife and son to New Zealand. I have been given Himank's room to sleep in, just as I was given the room of the emigrant daughter at Jay Pal's house.

As the sun rises in the sky, we move into the dining room, where we continue our conversation over breakfast around the large oval table. There is added excitement in the air, for a party of us is set-

ting out for the west today. After nearly three weeks in Kathmandu, I have developed a bad cough from the air pollution, and
Nava Raj has arranged a cure for me in the lake town of Pokhara,
resting below the Annapurna Massif.

Ten of us pile into the Land Cruiser with Kanak's older brother
Subarna at the wheel. I am the only non-Nepalese and notice that I
am also the only one who buckles my seatbelt. With much laughter
and well-wishing, we leave the rest of the family behind and drive
west out of the valley, taking the Prithvi Highway, built by the Chinese in the early 1970s.

When I was in Nepal in 1987, I traveled some distance on this
famous highway, and I remember it as the roughest ride I have ever
had. I was in a very old Mercedes bus then, one that had seen much
better days, driven by a talkative, near-toothless Nepali, who
derived pleasure from swinging wildly around hairpin curves and
huge rockslides and driving through deep potholes, missing the
oncoming traffic by inches.

Luckily, today I am in the front seat of a Land Cruiser, and Subarna, an even-tempered, handsome young father, is an experienced
and careful driver. Even so, it remains a wearying drive with the
assorted traffic moving as quickly as it can around countless sharp
curves and dodging suddenly to avoid potholes. I focus on the first-
class scenery of the Middle Hills and the deep gorges of the rushing
Trisuli River. I observe the villages—peasant settlements of a few
huts clustered neatly near the road.

We come to Mugling Bazaar, a rough town where the road,
nothing but huge ruts, is deliberately left unrepaired so that those
driving through will stop and partake of the local fare. Mugling, a
departure point for rafting on the Trisuli, is filled with prostitu-
tion, drugs and the cheapest hostelry. From my comfortable vantage point next to Subarna, I see a chaotic disarray of people

milling about the crowded market area, and I'm content to be moving on.

We continue west out into the clean countryside. Women in colorful garb bend to sweep the dirt paths in front of their huts with handmade brooms. Others walk in small groups, bent over from the weight of leafy branches or long straw on their backs, looking like walking haystacks. Men move slowly behind buffalo-drawn plows, women winnow the last of the rice crop, tossing the grain high in the air from their broad reed trays. Women gather at the village well, which is often simply an iron pipe projecting from a cement wall, and fill their water jugs—brass, tin, plastic. I see women sitting by the roadside, breaking up rocks with heavy stone hammers held with both hands and then pounding the stones into ever smaller pieces to make gravel.

We pass the road to Gorkha, home of King Prithvi Narayan Shah, the celebrated warrior who unified the clashing eighteenth-century tribes into what has become modern-day Nepal. Today Gorkha Durbar remains a fort with palace and temple perched high above the town in a perfect defensive posture to ward off invaders.

As we head into the afternoon sun, I catch glimpses of the snow-covered Himalaya behind the Middle Hills. These monumental mountains were left essentially untouched in their supreme beauty until the nineteenth century, when early adventurers risked their lives to attempt climbing the snow-clad peaks. As the technology of climbing developed, further expeditions were made in the twentieth century. I remember as a girl reading *Annapurna*, the story of the French expedition led in 1950 by Maurice Herzog, the first man to climb a mountain over eight thousand meters or twenty-six thousand feet high. This herculean adventure opened the way for other climbers around the world to attempt scaling the high peaks of the

Himalaya. The race was on until the summit of Mount Everest, the highest of all, was reached in 1953 by Edmund Hillary of New Zealand and his Sherpa guide, Tenzing Norgay.

I find something ghostly about the Himalaya on our drive west. Their bases concealed by clouds, they seem to rise out of nowhere, the snow-laden slopes, in an eerie game of hide and seek, appearing and disappearing in the mist. As we round a bend, they suddenly confront us, an immense silent presence demanding our respect.

Pokhara, our destination—with its hectic traffic, trash in the rutted streets and black smoke-spewing vehicles—seems to be just more of Kathmandu. But then Subarna deposits me at my hotel, The Lakeview Resort, where I am given the highest corner room with a view of the mountains and lake. I have landed in an inviting, restful spot and have Nava Raj to thank for it. I relax in the privacy of my new room and take the first leisurely hot bath I have had on the trip. I move out onto my courtyard balcony, pulling my sweater around me to keep warm in the chill night air. Through the trees I see, bathed in moonlight, the snow cloak of the mountain Machhapuchhare, regal in its stillness.

It is dark at five-thirty in the morning when Subarna and his cousins arrive to drive me up to the best vantage point to watch the dawn rise over the western Himalaya. I'm surprised to learn that though the cousins live here, no one in the family has taken part in this ritual before. We leave the broad fertile valley of Pokhara, completely quiet at this predawn hour, and wend our way up into the hills to Sarangkot, where the remains of an old fort rest at 5,223 feet. We walk the last of the way up a path of steep stone steps, and as on those final steps up Flower Mountain, my legs are reluctant.

Tourists in parkas and sunglasses have assembled with binoculars and cameras to witness and record the beginning of another day. A buzz of excitement stirs the crowd. Ahead of us, a mere twenty-five miles away, looms the Annapurna Massif. Even closer is Machhapuchhare, or Fishtail, so called because, from a certain angle to the west, it looks like the two-pronged tail of a fish. This peak, reserved for the hearts of the Nepalese and used proudly by them as an emblem, is not as high as the Annapurna Massif surrounding it, but unlike those peaks, which now earn big dollars for the Nepalese from foreign mountaineers and trekkers, Machhapuchhare is still honored as a holy mountain, and the Nepalese government refuses to grant permits to climb it.

The first pink rays of sun strike the highest peak, Dhaulagiri to the far west, then the Annapurna peaks in order of height: I, II, III and Annapurna South, as if a mighty magician were controlling the show with a wand. The splendid pyramid of Machhapuchhare, which appears the highest from my vantage point, yet is in fact the lowest, is the last to be found by the sun's rays. I am here just this one morning, watching the ritual of sunrise over the peaks, but I want to remember that this sign of renewal occurs every day. I want to carry the innocence of the morning's splendor in the highest mountains in the world with me.

In the last decades the western Himalaya have become as famous among climbers and trekkers as the eastern Himalaya around Mount Everest. Pokhara is the town from which Peter Matthiessen and the biologist George Schaller departed on their 250-mile trek to Crystal Mountain in the Land of Dolpo in search of the snow leopard and the rare Himalayan blue sheep. In 1973 when they set out with a tattered band of Sherpas and porters, this was still remote territory, but now Pokhara is a chief departure point for the flourishing industry of trekking and mountaineering. Trails that

Matthiessen and Schaller found barely passable are today filled with trekkers from all over the world. Hence the traffic and crowded streets I saw in town.

The Snow Leopard makes fascinating reading. Matthiessen describes the trip from Kathmandu to Pokhara, the same road I have just taken, in the misery of the late monsoon rains of September, the Trisuli River swollen to a brown flood. With no further roads to the west, his small party of Sherpas and porters began the arduous six-week trek in late fall to the illusive Crystal Mountain through dark gorges and around paths so narrow that a slip of the foot could mean death. Matthiessen and Schaller, both great lovers of the wilderness and the animals that inhabit it, were especially pleased that for weeks on end they did not hear a machine sound, so ancient was the technology of the villages they passed through. They became totally immersed in the diurnal cycle of life in the high Himalaya, which translates to "Abode of the Snow."

The other mountaineering book that captures my imagination here in Pokhara is Arlene Blum's *Annapurna: A Woman's Place*. It describes the American Women's Himalayan Expedition, which climbed Annapurna I in the fall of 1978. Blum mentions that she likes the name Annapurna, for it refers to the goddess of the harvest and roughly translates as "full of sustenance." I can relate to that, for when I saw the local women gathering bundles of rice in the golden fields of the surrounding countryside, I was witnessing the timelessness of Annapurna's legend. The text and photos of Blum's book document the thirteen women's harrowing adventure. Two hundred porters, each of whom carried a sixty-six-pound basket suspended from a tumpline across the forehead, accompanied the women to the base camp along with some twenty Sherpas, who served as guides. Two members of the expedition made history by being the first women to achieve the summit of Annapurna I, but two other women fell to their deaths in their attempt to conquer the harvest goddess's mountain.

While I admire tremendously the women's physical skill and mental courage and determination to make the climb, I find Matthiessen's approach the more appealing. Blum's story is all too human with its petty rivalries and intense desire to fulfill a goal at the expense of everything else. It is as if the Nepalese porters and Sherpas and the mountain itself became mere objects to be used for the purpose of achieving a personal goal. Matthiessen, philosophical by nature, treks for the journey itself. He, too, relates the human failings that become evident in the stress of his long mountain trek, but the rich experience of the journey is more important to him than the achievement of his goal. Matthiessen shows great sensitivity to the spirit of the place—the rock and snow of the Himalaya with their flora and fauna—and he has compassion and respect for the native peoples on whom he depends so completely for his survival. He seeks to understand the essence of these people, as expressed in their humor and their gods, monks and shrines, as if in knowing them, his own restless spirit will achieve some measure of peace.

As a Westerner in the crowd of foreign tourists watching the Himalayan sunrise, I catch a glimpse of the gulf between the modern commercial-technological cultures and an old culture still rooted in the natural-spiritual world. I see my Nepalese friends standing off to the side away from the foreign tourists clicking their cameras. I understand now why they have not come here before to see the dawn. I try to hold on to my belief in subjective relationships between people, subjective, because all of us and all creation are subjects, not objects to be used for selfish gain. The philosopher Martin Buber spoke of the "I-Thou" relationship, meaning that all people and all of nature—animals, trees, rocks—are related in a fundamentally spiritual way, which consists of mutual reverence.

One does not use the other. Mutual reverence is an ideal, to be sure, but nonetheless one that I long to achieve.

In the late afternoon sun, I walk solo along the lakeshore, enjoying the warmth and the reflection of Fishtail Mountain in Fewa Lake. I amble past booths of handmade crafts, and feeling rested and sentimental, I succumb to their charm. I buy a tablecloth, mats and a handsome vest, and then a good-looking handwoven cotton bag in which to carry my purchases.

As twilight falls, music hangs in the air, and I trace it to an open booth where a young flutist with wild black hair, looking irresistibly like the Hindu god Krishna enticing the maidens, is playing a sparkling melody on a wooden flute. I stop to talk to him. He tells me he is from Gorkha and that the flutes he is selling were all made there. He shows me how to hold the instrument and assures me I can learn to play it in three weeks. I ask him to play for me again, and he brings the instrument to life, his music spilling out into the night air. I choose a teakwood flute fitted with brass and tuck it into my new cloth bag.

In the evening I take dinner on the hotel terrace by the shore of the lake. The garden is festively lit with paper lanterns and has a stage where local dancers and musicians perform a cultural program. As I eat alone, my friendly young waiter peppers me with questions. Why am I alone? Why am I not married? How old am I? How do I have the money to travel so far from home? He estimates that my age is thirty-five, and I start to laugh. But then he tells me his mother is forty-six, "with many wrinkles, and she looks much older than you do." He is astonished when I tell him I am about to turn sixty. He explains that his mother has had a hard life and works long hours in the rice fields every day, and I tell him I work six hours a day inside an air-conditioned library.

My attention shifts to a table under the trees where the men, who have been drinking the strong wine, are singing and becoming a nuisance. Three men are dancing under the lanterns and shout to the others to join them. My waiter calls it a "police party." He says that the host has been charged with a crime and is bribing the police and their wives with an evening of entertainment so that he won't have to pay a fine and go to jail. The waiter shakes his head and says, "Too many police parties."

I leave the scene of dancers and drummers and besotted police and return to my room. From my balcony I watch the moon cast its spell upon the magic mountain, Machhapuchhare, the silver snow cone standing out handsomely against the black night sky. I think of the women of this place dominated by the massif named in honor of Annapurna, goddess of the harvest—the women who bring in the harvest, like the waiter's mother, their skin wrinkled and browned from decades of summer suns. And I remember the Western women who set their hearts on climbing the goddess's mountain, women who wanted to burst the bonds their society had put upon them.

These two groups are a twentieth-century study in contrast: the local women, part of an ancient agricultural people, working daily in the fields under the shadow of the mountain, praying to the goddess Annapurna for a good harvest to feed their families; the foreign women, using the mountain Annapurna as a giant hurdle to be conquered, proving to themselves and their society that they can overcome the limits they have inherited as women. Seated on my balcony, I ponder the diverse paths taken by the two cultures and admit that I, too, have undertaken my journey, in part, to prove my independence.

Chitwan
Pursuing the Horizon

I saw a man pursuing the horizon;
Round and round they sped.
I was disturbed at this;
I accosted the man.
"It is futile," I said,
You can never-"

"You lie," he cried,
And ran on.
—Stephen Crane, *The Black Riders and Other Lines*

rriving at Nepal's Royal Chitwan National Park after a tedious drive, never faster than forty kilometers (twenty-four miles) per hour over rutted and relentlessly curving roads, I step out of the Land Cruiser and walk to the bank of the Rapti River, which defines the border of the park. The only bridge in sight is a low-slung footbridge just wide enough for a person to push a bicycle across. Children are playing at the river's edge, a naked little boy is howling in tears for all he is worth, and an old jeep is fording the stream, sending waves up and down the banks.

The well-seasoned jeep driver throws my bag into the back of his vehicle, I climb aboard and the World War II Russian jeep plunges back into the river like a true amphibian. We emerge on the other side, and picking up speed, the driver barrels along the dirt paths, using the small rubber button on the steering wheel to beep the bleating horn and clear the way of chickens and children as we pass. It's impressive to see these nearly sixty-year-old wartime vehicles still performing in this jungle terrain.

In twenty minutes, we arrive at a small cluster of simple thatch-roofed cottages called The Jungle Resort. It feels good to come to a halt and to be rid of conveyances for a while. Davendra, the mild-mannered manager of the small resort, has promised my friends in Kathmandu that he will look after me, and he leads me to my cottage. I welcome the simplicity of the place—two single cots with mosquito netting hanging over them, a small table holding a pop bottle with a stub of a candle stuck in the neck, several hooks on the wall, and a bathroom with the bare essentials. I step out onto my little cement porch and breathe in the warm, clean air.

I am in a totally different environment, although, surprisingly, I can still see the white Himalaya one hundred miles away on the northern horizon. Life here is on a horizontal plane, not a vertical one. I am in the Terai, the hot, subtropical plain that is geographically a part of the Gangetic plain, whose rivers empty into the Bay of Bengal. Until the 1960s, this land was heavily forested and malarial, but since the draining of the swamps and a concerted effort to eradicate the mosquitoes in the 1950s, the area has become hospitable to human settlement. People have come south from the mountainous regions of Nepal and north from India, seeking a better way of life, farming in the fertile cleared land or working in the large factory towns. The open border with India allows free commerce, and as a result, the Terai has become the most populated and fastest growing area of Nepal.

Royal Chitwan National Park is the oldest national park in Nepal. It came into being in an effort to protect the big game animals—tigers, rhinos and elephants—that had been the prey of British and Nepalese aristocrats during the nineteenth century and first half of the twentieth, and the victims of poachers and new settlements in the fifties and sixties. An animal sanctuary was established in 1964—displacing twenty-two thousand people from the area. The park was founded in 1973. Since that time, the animal populations have recovered, the remaining indigenous Tharu (pro-

nounced TAHroo) continue to live in their villages, and the park
has become an attraction for visitors the world over.

One of the joys of taking a trip is swapping stories with other travelers. This evening at dinner I meet my fellow lodgers by candle-
light in the thatched-roof hut that serves as dining room. We are
seated under a fan, which hangs from the peak of the roof and is
powered by the kitchen generator behind the building. I had heard
the cook crank up the generator an hour before dinner, just long
enough for the kitchen staff to prepare the main meal of the day. A
lit candle on each of the two occupied tables throws off little halos
of light in the dim circular room.

My tablemates are John, a New Hampshire lawyer whom I
judge to be in his fifties; Jost, a Dutch student who has hooked up
with John on the road; and Joachim, a tall, blonde Swedish acrobat.
At the neighboring table are two vivacious Norwegian girls who
are law students on holiday, and a phlegmatic young Israeli couple.

I thoroughly enjoy the diversity of our little ensemble. John asks
me where I have traveled and is excited to hear that I have been
living in Nepalese homes. He and Jost met on a train in China and
then traveled through Tibet together. They say it is very rough
there, and they spent most of their energy trying to stay warm.
They resented that they had to pay high prices to the state-run
tourist agency to have the most rudimentary unheated accommo-
dations, where the bathroom was a hole in the ground across a stone
courtyard. Joachim, a large, peaceable young man who sips his soup
loudly, says he has stayed for several weeks at The Jungle Resort to
learn the stick dance, which the native Tharu people perform
locally. There is a performance this evening, and the three men ask
me if I would like to join them there.

After dinner, we walk over the dirt roads through the village of mud huts, which is remarkably quiet. I hear no machine noise, just a few children playing, the sound of crickets in the neighboring mustard fields and our own footsteps on the dirt. Without the omnipresent hum of engines and machines, I feel back in another time and think of my Pennsylvania grandmother, who used to walk to her local vegetable market with a basket over her arm and return home to cook large meals on her big coal stove. As we round a bend, an elephant saunters toward us down the middle of the path, carrying a large sheaf of straw in its trunk; this encounter jolts me back to southern Nepal.

The dance, or cultural program, is held in the village's dirt-floored assembly hall filled with rows of wooden benches. Waiting for the show to begin, I ask John about his life, what brings him here. He tells me he began his travels six years ago by taking a six-month leave of absence from his divorce and bankruptcy law practice, and he's been on the road ever since. As he speaks, he punches the air with his fists, and his face is knit into a frown. He enumerates the countries he has yet to see, as if ticking off items on a list of chores that must be done. Far from a carefree vagabond, he seems pursued by private demons who are constantly pushing him to see more and more new lands.

With a clatter of footsteps on the wooden platform, a drummer emerges in center stage, striking up a strong rhythm on his hand drum. He is followed by a dozen young barefoot men in their teens and early twenties, who begin circling around the drummer. They walk rhythmically, and then, raising their arms, begin a complex circle dance, using the sticks they hold as weapons against each other. In this Tharu war dance of intricate footwork and dexterous manipulation, the sticks clack loudly against each other as the men turn, bend, jump and leap around the circle in an increasing frenzy of warring gestures.

In the front row, I see Joachim, sitting in rapt attention, trying to take it all in. The men on the stage are dark, small in stature, very slim, with not a bit of flesh to spare. Joachim, the benign Swedish acrobat, is physically the antithesis of these men—tall, large-boned, fair-skinned—and I am curious as to why he is so smitten with this tribal war dance that he must learn it. On the walk to the performance he told me that he is not good at the dance, he gets hurt by the other men's sticks, and his large physique is an impediment to the agility required to compete with the slim bodies of the Tharu men. Nonetheless, Joachim perseveres in a blind resolve to overcome the odds against his becoming a Tharu stick dancer. His belief that he will never be good at the dance infuses him with melancholy, yet he is locked into a brute determination to try.

On our walk back to our cottages, lit by the radiance of the near-full moon and the pale little dancing circles from our flashlights, I think about John and Joachim and how both are caught in a kind of obsession they will most likely not be able to satisfy. It reminds me of Stephen Crane's poem, which I memorized as a girl, about pursuing the horizon, about stubbornly trying to accomplish something that is impossible. It is easy to observe others in actions that seem foolish or vain, but I ask myself now if I, too, like John and Joachim, am locked into futile patterns of my own making. Am I also trying to pursue the horizon?

Pondering the question, I answer that it took the act of divorce to finally break the long pattern of my own futile behavior. I remember often asking myself as a wife, if I had a good, bad, mediocre or excellent marriage, and I usually concluded that it was good, but never excellent, which is what I was striving for. When I look back now, I think I achieved only moderate success in what I wanted from the most important relationship in my life. I am an idealist and a romantic, and I chose to marry someone who turned out to be quite different from me. That in itself is not bad, but as the years went by, the differences between us increased, until a wide gap separated us. Despite the gap, I kept trying to bring the two of us together in an ideal marriage. Seen from my present vantage point, I think that I was engaged in a kind of futile behavior, but I couldn't see it at the time. I always thought that with more effort on my part, more patience, more determination, I would eventually succeed in having a richly creative, harmonious marriage.

Over the years I began to listen to others' comments about my marriage. People who knew my husband and me superficially tended to think we were an excellent couple. In some ways we were—particularly when we were united in a community or social effort. Those who knew us better would drop hints about our incompatibility—but I didn't want to hear them. Only in the last years of my marriage, when I was beginning to look out more for myself than for the relationship, could I acknowledge that we were not the ideal couple I was striving for us to be.

Once we reached a state of crisis, I was willing to try anything to save the marriage, but nothing worked. Perhaps my husband felt as helpless as I did, watching the collapse of our thirty-year union.

During that time, my children returned home for vacation from college, and one day they told me how they and their best friends across the street had characterized their respective parents. The neighbor kids had sketched their parents like this: "Al says to Mia: 'Mia, did you know the moon is made of green cheese?' And Mia replies, 'Oh, Al! You are so wonderful! Only you know that the moon is truly made of green cheese!'" Then my children sketched their parents: "Paul says to Nan: 'Nan, did you know that the moon is made of green cheese?' And Nan answers, 'Don't be ridiculous, Paul! Everyone knows that the moon is not made of green cheese!'"

This was a tough awakening for me. In a short anecdote, my

children had summed up how combative and negative, even unromantic, I had become. The recognition that I was not able to live a full, creative and harmonious life with my husband was the beginning of an eventual parting of the ways. And now, while Mia and Al, who have always been supportive of each other, are off in Scotland celebrating their thirty-fifth wedding anniversary with their children, I am seven years divorced and here in the jungle of Nepal on my own.

I awaken at six on my first morning in the national park, and feeling well rested, I prepare for the jungle walk. Yesterday I had overheard two guides saying to each other that they would rather be sitting on the back of an elephant if they were to meet a rhino than be on foot in the jungle, so I am a bit nervous about taking the walk. I'm wondering if at my age I would have the agility needed to dodge an enormous wild animal. At the same time, I can't imagine missing the opportunity to go.

Ram (pronounced Rom), a friendly, young Tharu who has studied biology and speaks excellent English, is to be my guide while I am here. He meets me in the courtyard, and we join my walking companions: David, a friendly, eager nineteen-year-old from Australia, and Isaac and Ruth, the Israeli couple. Rom, wearing the jungle-green uniform of the park guides, asks Isaac to please change his bright red shirt because it will act as a target for the rhinos. Laughing at the idea of it, Isaac says he has no other shirt (I wonder what is in the large backpack I saw him carry into his cottage), so Ram has no choice but to lead us in a fast-paced walk to a point at the edge of the jungle where we meet our professional jungle guide, Romesh. Also a young Tharu, Romesh is dressed in a camouflage jacket and good hiking boots, and carries a staff. Ram wears flip-flops and also carries a stick. The two converse in their native Tharu language, and I surmise it must be about Isaac's shirt.

Romesh immediately takes charge, and we set out, single file, through the elephant grass (as high as an elephant), walking at a swift pace. The Tharus use their legs for basic transportation, so they walk easily and efficiently. We come to a small stream that is bridged by a single log, ten feet long, and one by one we walk across. I wait till the younger ones have gone first—Isaac looks annoyed, but shakily walks the log—then I steady myself like a high-wire artist, and putting one foot in front of the other, walk the length of the log.

As we are about to enter the jungle, Romesh gathers us in a small circle and gives us a serious talk about the endangered one-horned rhinos, saying that they are large wild animals and have killed people. Since we are entering their territory, we must know how to protect ourselves, should a rhino charge. Romesh's advice : 1) Climb the nearest tree. 2) Find a large tree (not easy to do) and play hide and seek with the rhino, always staying on the other side of the tree. 3) Run in a zigzag line, not straight. Rhinos have great stamina and can run forty kilometers without stopping, so it is impossible to outrun them. 4) Throw anything you are carrying—bag, camera— in another direction to confuse the rhino.

I am startled by this little speech and begin praying I will not see a rhino on this jungle walk. Isaac, however, pooh-poohs these instructions, and from the start I can see a standoff coming between Romesh, who understands and respects the ways of the jungle, and Isaac, the cynical, big-city man. Hearing about the rhinos reminds me of the snakes I know are here, also—pythons, king cobras and green pit vipers—so I am determined to walk with care, watching where I place my feet. I wonder if the snakes are watching for me as well!

We move into the jungle of kapok and rhino trees (trees big enough to climb when you see a rhino coming) in silence. Romesh and Ram set a quick pace, and David and I follow, soon leaving Isaac and Ruth behind. We watch how Romesh cocks his head for sounds and keeps his eyes alert for any movement. Several times he stops, and with the ease of a monkey, he or Ram climbs a tree to scout for rhinos. We hear one bellowing in the distance, and we even come across a huge pile of rhino dung, still steaming in the cool morning air, but we cannot see the rhino itself. We wait for Isaac and Ruth to catch up and then resume walking, our eyes following the narrow path lit by sunlight filtering through the trees.

Romesh stops when he sees birds and identifies them quietly—a few parakeets, jungle fowl crossing our path, a brilliant wild peacock that takes off at our approach. The park contains over four hundred species of birds, so it is a paradise for birders. Farther on, Romesh comes to a halt and points through the trees. A herd of chital deer, looking like spotted fawns, is grazing. I could never have found them myself, their camouflage is so good. When we take a five-minute rest stop, I ask Romesh how he knew the deer were there, and he says he noticed the movement of a few leaves. He tells us that the monkeys and the deer travel together, having common enemies in the big cats, and each gives a warning signal to the other when danger is near. I marvel at how observant Romesh is, and as if to confirm my thoughts, he spots blood on David's white sock: a fat black leech has made David's ankle home.

Romesh spills over with lore of the jungle, yet Isaac, standing tall and aloof from the group, remains cynical. Then Romesh turns to him and asks him to climb the nearest tree to scout for rhinos. Isaac just laughs. Romesh insists, saying it is his turn to scout. Isaac walks over to the tree and, being much larger than Romesh and Ram, easily takes hold of the lowest branch. But, like Joachim trying to learn the Tharu stick dance, Isaac soon finds that his larger physique is not as agile as the natives'. He makes many attempts to gain a foothold, but in vain. Then he gives up, cursing and claiming the tree is too slippery to climb. Romesh smiles and scampers up the tree like a monkey; Isaac remains silent for the rest of the four-hour walk.

David and I take advantage of Romesh's knowledge of the jungle, bombarding him with questions. He tells us he leads seven-to ten-day camping trips into the jungle. He loves to go deep into the sal forest where the Bengal tigers and leopards live. They are sleeping now in the light of day. Romesh asks David and me if we have noticed the electricity line in the village; he is disturbed by this new addition. He believes his people should keep to their old ways and not embrace modern technology. He sees a clear path for himself, working as a jungle guide and helping to preserve the traditional ways of the Tharu. Ram, too, talks about his people's customs and says he hopes to marry a local girl and remain a park guide.

We never do see a rhino on our jungle walk, and I'm not the least bit disappointed. When we return to the open fields, I thank Romesh and Ram warmly for their expert guidance. It is refreshing for me to see two young men who are not looking elsewhere for quick riches, but have found meaningful work in preserving the ways of their land and people.

I rise again at six, and this morning I take time to savor the quiet. When I step outside my cottage, I look a hundred yards to my right and see a steady line of villagers walking or bicycling on the dirt road, but I hear only wisps of their chatter on the light morning breeze. A bullock cart follows, but it, too, is quiet with its old rubber truck tires moving over the dirt.

By seven I am following Ram along dirt paths through dewy fields of mustard and hay to the river. A small group of park visitors has assembled near three canoes along the shore. The Tharu boatman, holding his canoe in place with a pole on the shallow river bottom, says clearly, "Balance very important," as five of us step, one by one, into the center of the slender dugout canoe. We are surprised at how unstable it is in the water. I am sitting to the front, directly behind Ram, and watch as local people board other canoes and remain standing with their packages and bicycles as the canoes cross the fairly broad river without a wobble or a ripple.

Gradually we outsiders find our balance, and the canoe begins moving smoothly down the river, the boatman poling us in silence through the morning mist. We are here to look for the gharial, a crocodile native to these parts, as well as to bird watch. Gliding midriver, we look carefully at the grassy banks until we are able to spot the forequarters of a gharial, poking his head out of his small cave into the light, his long, thin snout just barely visible. We float effortlessly downstream, seeing two kingfishers, Indian rollers and, high overhead, a serpent eagle. The roughly hewn, yet sleek canoe serves us well on our river trip. Ram tells us it takes ten days for the Tharu men to carve a canoe from a tree trunk.

When we disembark Ram and I continue our walk at a good clip past fields of cattle raised for their milk and curd. Half an hour later we arrive at the park's famous elephant breeding camp, where mothers and babies are kept in a protected area in an effort to increase the stock. Off in a shaded part of the forest, we find six mothers and several babies in a special enclosure. I notice the bundles of rice, molasses and salt, wrapped and tied with long leaves of grass. An adult elephant consumes thirty-five of these nutritious bundles a day.

I attend a lecture and learn that it takes two years to train an ele-

phant. Once a handler, or *mahout,* has worked with a particular elephant, he remains with that animal for the duration of its life. The
mahout, sitting on the elephant's neck with his legs behind the
animal's ears, uses universal verbal commands and leg signals to
direct the elephant to turn left or right, back up, lie down, and so
on. Elephants are intelligent, and the commands can be quite
sophisticated, such as, "push the object with your feet" or "push the
object with your head."

I remember Ushan, one of my students from Sri Lanka, telling
me years ago that if the handlers of his family's elephants treated
them well, they would give loyal, lifelong service. Part of the daily
routine was to take the elephants to the river to play after they had
put in a good day's work. But if the trainers worked the elephants
beyond their capacity or abused them in any way, they could turn
with destructive force upon whatever was within their reach.

Wanting to get closer to the huge, agreeable animals, I volunteer
to mount a female elephant named Brunkali. I step with my right
foot into the curve of her lowered trunk; then as I face her and hold
onto her ears, she swats me over her head onto her back, as if I were
nothing more than a piece of popcorn. I am momentarily disoriented and grab the few long, black hairs on her tough, leathery hide
to pull myself in place. Once upright and straddling her solo at the
neck, I feel victorious and can't stop smiling.

Late in the afternoon, I join others at the elephant mounting sta-
tions in the cool of the forest and wait my turn to climb the steps of
the platform, then sit in the left rear corner of the *haudah*, a large
wooden seat with a railing that is strapped like a saddle to the elephant. This is the beginning of the much-anticipated elephant
safari into the jungle of early evening.

At first, I have to learn how to sit and hold onto the wooden railing of the haudah so that I don't slide into my fellow passengers or feel as if I am sliding off the elephant. When I find a comfortable position, what I like best about the ride is the rhythmic swish, the long, graceful strides of the elephant, who walks in a steady, unhurried pace. We emerge silently from the trees onto the riverbank, where the elephant steps easily into the river, the water rising nearly to her shoulders. All the while she continues her rhythmic stride, making the quiet stream suddenly sound like an ocean.

We reach the other side, and the elephant climbs onto the bank and proceeds down a path. Entering the tall grass on the back of the elephant, I feel secure when we come upon a mother rhino grazing with her baby. We stop and watch the pair, the mother not pleased that we have come this close to her baby. She watches us nervously until we move on.

The safari continues, and the elephant enters the jungle of tall trees and dense undergrowth. I watch the patches of sky become smaller as we head deeper into the tropical forest. Though the path we follow is barely visible to me, the elephant seems sure of her way. Overhead I hear the commotion of langur monkeys swinging from branch to branch, while my elephant continues at the same even pace, *swish, swish,* brushing large branches aside as if they were mere sticks. We follow a crisscross of jungle paths with no visible markings, and I lose all sense of direction. I concentrate on the wildlife—birds, monkeys, deer and more rhinos roaming the cool shade under the jungle cover.

When we finally emerge from the forest into the elephant grass, the full moon is rising. The river lies ahead, and I can see the snowy chain of the Himalaya on the northern horizon. The deep blue of the evening sky forms a glorious backdrop to Nepal's amazing range of environments—from the Arctic temperatures of snow-clad peaks reaching miles into the sky to the sub-tropical breezes and tall grass I am moving through now.

The elephant steps into the river, creating her own rhythmic waves as she walks. I take a deep breath, trying to hold onto all the sounds and smells and sights of this moment. I nod to the full moon, and I'm quite sure the moon nods back to me.

Himalaya
Everest

I am a lucky man. I have had a dream, and it has
come true.

—Tenzing Norgay, *Tiger of the Snows*

The jet stream swirling around Mount Everest is so fierce
that my flight has been delayed. Fog has socked us in at
the airport in Kathmandu with visibility down to a few
feet, and unless conditions improve, my flight will be canceled. I'm
sipping hot tea in the upstairs airport café with Nirmal, the right-
hand man of Somendra, while waiting for The Mountain Flight, the
famous one-hour plane ride that flies east as close as possible along
the chain of the Himalaya to view Mount Everest from the air. The
prized ticket, fought for by tourists from around the globe and too
expensive for most Nepalese, is a gesture of hospitality from
Somendra, who had accepted my hospitality years ago as a student
in America.

Looking out the window into the fog, I recall the story of the
1996 expeditions on Everest, when eight people died and others suffered grave injury in a sudden storm that raged on the summit,
making the descent for the climbing parties nearly impossible. Not
long ago I heard David Breashears, the filmmaker, speak about that
ill-fated journey—he was there with his Imax crew, filming *Everest*
at the time. Speaking to a capacity audience, Breashears said he

wasn't the only one on the mountain who questioned the wisdom of the expeditions pressing on, disregarding nature's warning signals. He said that hubris had taken hold of some of the climbers, who were determined at all costs to achieve their goal of reaching the summit. This hubris, he felt, was responsible for the tragedy.

I pour myself a second cup of tea. Hubris, the pride that brings down humans in daring endeavors. The Greeks told the story of Icarus, mythic hero, who, wanting to soar through the heavens, flew so close to the sun that the wax on his wings melted and he fell to his death in the Aegean. Americans remember the twentieth-century captain of the *Titanic,* who, wanting to flaunt the technology of his new ship, led his trusting passengers into the iceberg night and disaster in the North Atlantic. Icarus felt himself to be invincible, the captain felt his manmade vessel to be indestructible. Both, like the climbers on that fateful journey up Everest, underestimated the power of nature. Hubris: excessive pride, arrogance, human determination gone one step too far. Am I, like Icarus, about to fly too close to the mountain?

Flying too close to the mountain is what introduced me, as a child, to death. I was five years old, sitting at the dinner table with my family, when a loud knock on the front door disturbed our meal. My father rose from the table, unlatched the lock and opened the door. A Western Union messenger handed him a telegram. Reluctantly, my father read the lines typed across the page. "Howard's dead," he said, his eyes welling with tears. Howard was my father's younger brother, my uncle and beloved godfather, who was a doctor and pilot stationed in England in the Army Air Corps. In the following weeks we learned that my uncle had been piloting a planeload of wounded soldiers from France to Ireland and, while attempting to fly over the Isle of Man, had crashed the plane into a cloud-covered mountain. It was July 4, 1944. He was twenty-nine years old and the only one on the plane who was killed.

That moment at the dinner table was my first contact with death. I struggled to understand that my uncle Howe, even taller and more handsome than my father, would never return to hold me in his arms, to tell me stories of his travels, to bring me another present. Seeing his name added, in gold letters, to the list in the town park of war heroes who had died for their country did not assuage my grief. I lived with a sadness and a longing I had not known before. When I gradually realized that some day I, too, would die, I became all the more determined to live my life to the fullest.

I thought I had worked through the shock of my uncle's death when I was a girl, but it continued to haunt me in a new way when I became a mother. Many years later, as my son grew into boyhood and then manhood, I began to discern in him a great resemblance to my uncle. Their eyes and hair were the same color. When Peter would tell a joke, his smile of amusement reminded me of my uncle. When my son reached his full height of six feet, four inches, it was the same height as my uncle Howe. Leafing through old family photos, I found a picture of my uncle relaxing on a blanket on the ground at a picnic: his posture was identical to my son's.

Seeing the outward similarities between my uncle and my son led me to believe the two were connected in a deeper way. I began a secret dialogue with God, praying that my son would not die young, as my uncle had. I prayed especially that there would be no war in which he would have to fight. I promised myself that when Peter celebrated his thirtieth birthday, the jinx of an early death would be gone, and my son would be home free.

Only after Peter died at twenty-two could I see that all my worry had done no good, all my prayers for his long life had been in vain. Whereas my uncle's death had introduced me to the natural course of life and death, my son's death confirmed for me the existence of a greater force far beyond my control. Even though my prayers had not been answered, I did not lose faith. Instead I saw myself within a much greater frame of reference than ever before. I understood that I was infinitesimal in a cosmos beyond all comprehension.

The loudspeaker crackles with the announcement that my plane has been given clearance to depart, even though the winds around Everest are raging at two hundred knots per hour. Nirmal waves good-bye to me as I climb the steps of the twin-engine plane, one of three women among fifteen passengers. I sit down by the window and say a silent prayer that my pilot, who holds the lives of his passengers in his hands, has the wisdom not to taunt the power of the jet stream.

Being a pilot in Nepal is an honored profession, and only the best pilots are chosen for this flight. Thinking of my safety, Somendra has chosen the best seat on the best airline for me. I am directly behind the pilot's cabin and have an excellent vantage point into the cockpit.

We climb quickly away from Kathmandu, leaving the swarming population of the valley behind. Our small plane curves up in an eastward arc, then straightens to fly a parallel course along the austere no-man's-land of the snow-clad mountains. I am the first passenger invited into the cockpit, and standing behind the pilot, I watch him indicate the direction of flight, naming the peaks along the way. Ganesh Himal represents the elephant-headed god of good luck and prosperity. Langtang Lirung reigns over Langtang National Park. The double summit of Gauri Shankar is named after the Hindu god Shiva and his consort, Gauri. The Nepalese call Everest Sagarmatha, or Brow of the Oceans, referring to the epoch when the earth was covered with seas except for the summit of Sagarmatha, which rose as a brow above the waters. It is the West that appropriated for the highest mountain the name of Sir George

Everest, who led the British Survey of India team that first meas-
ured the mountain's height in 1852.

There are three ranges of the Himalaya, and on this flight we are
following the line of the Great Himalaya, the range that encom-
passes the world's highest peaks. As we move toward Everest, the
mightiest mountain of them all stands out among the snow-covered
cones, not only because of its superior height, but because of the
exposed black granite of its windblown southwestern face and the
tell-tale plume of snow storming from the summit to the east. I
watch intently as the spume of snow, just a few miles from me, is
blown in a great white sheet, borne away on the most powerful
winds I have ever seen. Here the wind is not the friendly element I
have so often courted, but a terrifying power, the jet stream—which
normally travels above the earth—touching down on the planet's
highest peak, whipping up a havoc of its own. I wonder how close
we can go without being drawn into the vortex of swirling air.

What must it have been like for the early climbers to strike out into
the uncharted frozen peaks of the Himalaya? I try to imagine the
sense of discovery that Edmund Hillary and Tenzing Norgay experienced on that vivid day in May 1953 when they succeeded, against terrifying odds, as the first human beings to reach the summit of Everest.

I am partial to Tenzing Norgay, the Sherpa guide, whose homeland lay beneath Everest. In his Tibetan-Sherpa language, he called
the highest mountain Chomolungma, Mother Goddess of the World.
In *Tenzing of Everest,* Norgay is quoted as saying before he reached
the summit, "I offer everything, my very life, to Chomolungma—she
will preserve me." Just as I have struggled to fathom my place within
the greatness of creation, I see my fellow being, Tenzing Norgay,
grappling with his place in the scheme of things when he offers to
give his life to the Mother Goddess, the very mountain whose
summit he hopes to embrace.

Norgay did reach the summit, of course, and described in *Tiger of the Snows* what it felt like to stand on the highest peak of the world:

> I looked down the long way we ourselves had come . . . and on to the valleys and hills of my homeland. Beyond them, and around us on every side, were the great Himalayas, stretching away through Nepal and Tibet . . . the whole sweep of the greatest range on earth . . . under the spreading sky. It was such a sight as I had never seen before and would never see again: wild, wonderful and terrible.

I watch out the window as our plane makes a slow U-turn, just beyond Mount Everest, and then passes slowly before the granite wall, allowing me to come as close as I will ever be to the highest point on earth. Suspended in the air before Mount Everest, I watch the snow being swept like stardust up into the royal blue sky, as if some giant godly servant were determined to keep the stone surface of the world's highest mountain bare for all to see, defining the wild and wonderful realm of the Mother Goddess of the World.

Nagarkot
Death and the Morning Star

> Snow mountains, more than sea or sky, serve as a
> mirror to one's own true being, utterly still, utterly
> clear, a void, an Emptiness without life or sound
> that carries in Itself all life, all sound.
> —Peter Matthiessen, *The Snow Leopard*

Kanak is good company driving down the Arniko
Highway. I am grateful to him for convincing his well-
meaning parents, in whose home I have been staying,
that I will not be lonely by myself in Nagarkot, high on the rim of
Kathmandu Valley. Being alone is considered an unhappy state in
many cultures of the world, and Kanak's parents want to make sure
I am well cared for. Allowing their foreign visitor to be alone seems
inhospitable to them.

On the Arniko Highway to Tibet, we pass the medieval town of
Bhaktapur and continue up the precipitous, winding road to
Nagarkot. At seven thousand feet, Nagarkot was once the site of a
fort—*kot* means fort—guarding the entrance to Nepal from Tibet.
Today it is best known as the place to view the dawn rising over the
full scope of the Great Himalaya. Kanak delivers me to my rustic
hotel, and after correcting confusion regarding my gender—I am
staying alone, so the reservations clerk assumed I was a man—he
bids me a cheerful farewell and heads over to the army barracks
nearby to spend the night with a friend.

Once settled in my cottage, I realize I am hungry and walk up the hill to the handsome brick lodge. I take a delicious Nepali meal, served buffet style, in the dining room and sit at a table near the tall windows where I have a view of the Himalaya veiled in evening mist. I enjoy the warmth and camaraderie of the lodge and explore the bookshelves before leaving. Slowly I walk back to my cottage, down steep and winding brick steps, pulling my Nepalese cashmere shawl around my shoulders to ward off the chill. The cool air and moist clouds I met on Pulchowki are here, too, sheltering me from the workaday world far below.

Standing on my private balcony, I watch the clouds fill the valley beneath me, shrouding the Himalaya. Even so, I sense the immensity behind the veil and pause to take in the serene beauty of the scene. Hardly a breath of air stirs, and all is silent in this numinous hour between day and night. Time slows down as I watch the twilight dissolve into dusk.

I know of no better way to articulate this moment than the poem "Wanderer's Evening Song" ("*Wandrers Nachtlied*") by Germany's greatest writer, Goethe. As a youth hiking in the Alps, Goethe had paused one evening in a mountain hut to record a few lines on the wall, describing what he felt. His words are so perfectly married to the German language that they do not translate successfully, yet the thought is universal: the peace settling over the mountaintops at dusk, after the birds have ceased singing in the forest, reminds us of our own mortality, that soon we, too, will be at rest.

This was one of my son's favorite poems—he had lived in Germany as a student and spoke German well—and I had requested a friend to read the poem at his funeral in St. David's Church, where he had grown up in the mountains of North Carolina. Later, when I attended Peter's memorial service at Yale, planned by his fellow students, I was astonished and deeply moved to hear that same

Goethe poem sung in a tenor voice as pure as the clearest crystal. Tears streamed down my face as I sat in the chapel, listening to Peter's friend sing. I feel tears falling now, not out of loneliness, as Kanak's parents had feared, but out of tenderness for the moment, for the quiet beauty before me that recalls the loss of my son.

When I try to think back on my son's life, what I remember are isolated incidents, flashes of memory, like snapshots in a photo album. I can see him as a baby, wrapped in his white sheepskin in the winter sun, watching the loons dive into the icy Fox River and emerge with a gleeful cry into the Wisconsin winter sky. I remember him in his deep blue snowsuit, reaching up to open the snow-covered mailbox to send his grandmother a drawing. I can hear the splash of his first dive into the aquamarine water of the big outdoor swimming pool in Germany. I can see him laughing with his sister, flying red kites on his birthday in a park out west. I remember watching him jog along the beach on Lake Michigan, wearing his Walkman and listening to *Chariots of Fire*. I can see his tall frame, reaching to catch a Frisbee while playing with his friends on spring break. I remember watching him eat lobster—without the bib—in a seafood restaurant in New Haven.

I think a mother's tremendous sense of loss that accompanies the death of her child comes from the severing of the thread of life, from the abrupt termination of the tangible, visible person the mother has nurtured from the day of conception. It is an irreparable loss. But in compensation for the physical loss of a child, I believe there are spiritual gains.

After Peter was gone, I realized I had been privileged to see the full arc of his life, from birth to death. Normally a mother does not see the end of her child's life. The child's arc is left open, unfinished, a question, when she dies, just as the beginning of her parents' lives is a mystery, a question. A mother cannot know the full span of her own life: the beginning and the ending are veiled from her consciousness. Yet I had glimpsed the full arc of my son's life and felt comfort in that. Burying his ashes was a ritual not unlike the evening rite of tucking him in bed as a child, only this time, it was for eternity.

Sometimes it seems as if the dead are as much with us as the living. Standing here alone in the Himalayan dusk, I feel very close to Peter's spirit. I can even connect to his lighter side—his witty sense of humor. Though he is no longer present for me in physical form, his spirit, which is timeless and without bounds, sustains me in ways far beyond the physical realm.

The time surrounding Peter's death was, without question, the saddest and most chaotic period of my life. My husband, Paul, and I were stunned to receive the call with the news of our son's death— it was incomprehensible that Peter, whom we had bantered with happily in a long phone conversation the night before, was dead. When the director of the Yale student health service hung up, we called Peter's number to see if he would answer the phone, but all we heard was his answering machine, giving the simple message "I'm not here right now." Weeks passed before we were told that his death was most likely due to cardiac arrhythmia, sudden death that leaves no physical trace behind. "Your son was in perfect health," the medical examiner in Connecticut said, after the autopsy.

Those early days of trying to assimilate the death of my son, who had been looking toward such a bright future, were painful in the extreme. I struggled to accomplish the simplest tasks, feeling clumsy and forgetful. My mind was constantly preoccupied, replaying the events of the days surrounding Peter's death in a loop that had no end. It was a trial, daily, just to keep going, for my body was completely out of balance. I was very hungry, but couldn't finish eating what was on my plate. I was always thirsty. I was exhausted, yet so high strung that I could sleep only in snatches. My nerves were shot—totally raw, like frayed electrical cords. I was disoriented. I dreamt I was on a train, a good train on a smooth track, riding through beautiful country. All of a sudden the train came to a complete halt, yet I was still moving ahead, down the track, alone, out in the open air without the train. I couldn't stop.

I struggled to reconfigure our family of four. We had been a square, a perfect square: father, mother, son, daughter. A four-starred constellation that made a beautiful circle. A mandala. Now one of the cardinal points was gone. Totally gone. I tried to force the square to become a triangle, but I couldn't figure out how. Was Peter's point really gone, or was he still with us? How could I draw this? Our family geometry was off. When we sat at the dinner table, his place was empty. His side of the table was vacant. But I continued to light all four candles.

In grieving and recovering from the death of our son, my husband and I took different paths. Paul struggled to find out exactly how Peter died, how the body of a healthy twenty-two-year-old could suddenly cease to function. He questioned doctors and scientists and read tirelessly in search of an answer. Beyond the medical examiner's report, I could not join my husband in his search. It was a fact that my son had died, and it was all I could do to accept that fact. I had to concentrate on the basics of getting out of bed in the morning and putting one foot in front of the other to move forward. I was worried about my daughter and struggled to find ways to be present for her. My lack of interest in tracing the scientific cause of Peter's death somehow indicated to Paul that I was unconcerned and aloof. Neither of us could understand the other's point of view.

Easter morning arrived, and the cold, clear air spoke for the first time of hope. Attending service with a lifelong friend in Duke Chapel was like rejoining humanity. People were talking, as in the marketplace, trying to be heard over the swelling crescendo of the organ. Preachers spoke in abrasive, nagging voices, but I listened when I heard a voice of calm, of strength, speaking of grief. Grieving comes naturally, the man's voice said. We need no lessons. Everyone experiences grief, thus we need not feel sorry for ourselves. I left the chapel and felt the weight upon me lighten, not entirely, but noticeably. I felt taller. I looked at Paul and saw that he was crying. He kissed me on the cheek. My friend Elli suggested that our family geometry was now a triangle with Peter in the middle. I liked the thought and told my daughter, Ellen. She liked it, too.

Over time, I was able to discover that I valued my own life as much as the life of my son. One bright morning, sitting on a sunny bank by the creek that flowed past my home, I was struck by the beauty of the day. It was early summer, and the fragrance of honeysuckle, the golden hues of day lilies, the rich greens coloring the woods, and the clear water rolling over the smooth brown stones— all that beauty joined to rekindle a spark at the core of my being. It was the spark that fueled my own love of life. With that small epiphany I knew I had to regain my balance and make the most of the time I had yet to live. This seems to have been the turning point, the moment when I was able to begin discarding the extreme sorrow of loss, the anger, the disbelief, the hopelessness, and start rebuilding my life.

Slowly I resumed discipline in my daily activities. I made myself adhere to a reasonable schedule of regular meals and bedtime. I continued working in the library, no matter how much my body ached. I was no longer embarrassed when tears spilled down my cheeks while I was working at the reference desk; I just took out one of my mother's linen handkerchiefs that I carried in my pocket and wiped the tears away. I did special favors for myself, as friends had done for me immediately after Peter's death. I copied my favorite poems of Emily Dickinson and Dylan Thomas and memorized them, reciting them aloud in the car as I drove to and from work. I drove the long way home, the back route over dirt roads and through the woods, sometimes stopping by the river to watch the water in its ever-flowing course. I always had tea at four o'clock, sitting on the screened porch by the creek, stroking our cat, Tristan, who purred softly, seeming to need me as much as I needed him.

The evening sky over the Himalaya fades in one long diminuendo into hushed darkness, pianissimo. I wait, wrapped in my cashmere, stroking the strands of the brown goats' wool. I hug myself to keep warm, to feel loved. I wait, as in a primordial Quaker meeting out in the open air, the dome of sky encircling me. I feel the pulse of my blood, am conscious of my breathing. The things that keep me alive.

Inside the cottage, I turn up the flame on my oil stove. I wash quickly in the stone bathroom, the marble feeling smooth and cold on the soles of my feet. I change to a nightgown and light the candle on the nightstand. I pull up the quilt around me in bed and open the book of Krishnamurti's writing that I found in the lodge after dinner.

> Thought has to stop. And it stops when you see beauty, something like a vast range of mountains with snow-covered peaks. The majesty of it, the grandeur of it takes you over.

Thought has to stop. Words have to vanish. Sleep must come.

I awake at the first pale light of day. My cottage room feels cozy, warmed by the oil stove, which has been burning through the night. Drops of moisture have condensed on the outside of the window-panes, lending an intricate design to the glass.

I slip into my raincoat and sandals, turn the lock slowly on my door, and step noiselessly onto the balcony where, just a short time before, I had watched the evening light fade, ever so gradually, into darkness. Now the darkness, just as slowly, is dissolving into light. The Chinese speak of *yin*, the feminine cosmic principle—moon, shade, night—and *yang*, the masculine cosmic principle—sun, light, day. Two aspects of one whole. Darkness and light. Death and life. Destruction and creation. The ebb and flow, ever evolving, ever changing in each of us, in all things. The world is utterly silent. Not a sound is heard, not a leaf stirs in the predawn stillness.

The first instant of seeing the panorama of the highest snow mountains in the world, from Dhaulagiri in the west to Everest in the east, sends a flash of fear through me. I am startled by the immensity of these giants of earth, who, only hours before, had hidden coyly behind a veil of clouds. The mountains are surprisingly close, yet remote and aloof. But just as the darkness dissolves into light, so my fear modulates into awe. The Great Himalaya, standing clear in the morning air, in regal calm, arouse in me a reverence, as if the Old Testament God Himself were appearing before me. I begin to understand why early peoples, still intimately tied to their land and natural surroundings, perceived high mountains with awesome dread as the home of the gods, why mountain peoples have spun myriad legends of the deities who inhabit their hills. "I will lift up mine eyes unto the hills, from whence cometh my help."

I close my eyes and listen to the power of the silence. I remember reading in Irina Tweedie's remarkable *Daughter of Fire* that so many yogis and spiritual seekers have meditated in the Himalaya—reciting the mantra *Om Mani Padme Hum*—that the mountains resound with the primeval syllable *Om*, representing the divine power of God, a drone in the key of D, emanating from deep within. Without uttering a sound myself, yet focusing on the key of

D, I add my inner voice to all the others who have chanted here through the ages.

My eyes scan the sky for stars. I am looking for the morning star, remembering Father Rivers calling out, giving hope to the crowd assembled for the funeral in St. David's on that cold March day. "Peter is the morning star!" It was an echo from the Revelation of Saint John the Divine. "I am the root and the offspring of David, and the bright and morning star." I see a sparkling near the horizon, perhaps Venus, and I call it my morning star. A point of light that signifies the presence of my son.

I look to the east toward dawn, where very slowly the light grows a tinge brighter, accentuating the vastness of the expanse before me. The white of the mountains softens to shades of blue, then violet, a palette of colors that delights even my untrained eye. Gradually the first shades of pink strike one high peak, then another, each peak beginning to glow separately, the pinks slowly melting into gold.

Below my cottage, very quietly, a door opens and closes. A rooster calls down in the village. A crow emerges from the tall trees beneath me, then another, and another, and they set out in free flight across the expanse of valley, their black wings soaring on the morning currents of air. Little by little the silence fills with a crescendo of morning sounds, as life awakens on this small plot of earth. To the east near Everest, the halo of golden light continues to grow and accumulate force until it bursts in full splendor, the new day's sun, rising above the Abode of the Snow. I can look only for a moment before the sun becomes blinding; then I turn toward the west to watch vast hues of color spreading down the white fields of snow, painting the mountains as far as my eyes can see.

The beauty of these snow peaks rings in prayerful music. The sounds in my head are familiar: the lush harmonies of a great orchestra; the timbre of the trumpet Peter played as a boy; the rising chords of a chapel organ; the sweet, melancholy refrain of Indira's voice, singing of love and loss, and the tolling of a brass bell, the tones vanishing into the air as surely and easily as our lives dissolve, one by one, into the great beyond.

New Delhi
Among Exiles

The place to find is within yourself.
—Joseph Campbell, *The Power of Myth*

I am sitting in the left-hand front passenger seat in a fast car, traveling along wide thoroughfares through New Delhi. Each time we stop at a major intersection, beggars thread their way through traffic and knock on the driver's window, holding out open palms, eyes imploring. The young prince, who is driving, reaches into the car's ashtray, pulls out several shiny coins, unrolls the window a few inches and drops a coin into each cupped palm. The eyes outside the glass mellow in thanks, the traffic light turns green, and we drive on through crowded streets to the next intersection.

My introduction to New Delhi comes courtesy of two banished Bhutanese princes who have lived much of their lives in this city, but who share my status as outsider. Former students at my university, Jurme, the elder prince, and Namgay, his younger brother, welcome me with genuine Asian hospitality. They are sons of former Bhutanese king Jigme Dorje Wangchuck, now deceased, and his second wife, who runs the family home in exile with the sureness of a queen. The house here in New Delhi is so full of photographs and keepsakes from the family's early life in Bhutan that I feel as if I have stepped into the Himalayan kingdom itself.

The story from my Bhutanese student princes is one of persecution and banishment, years ago, by the present king, then a young lad of seventeen and the elder half-brother of Jurme and Namgay. When their father died in 1972 on safari in Africa, his second wife by his side, the princes tell me that the first queen, back in Bhutan, engineered the exile of their mother and all her relatives. Things haven't changed much over the years. The present king and his ministers have repeatedly denied the exiles' requests for reentry into their homeland.

The house that serves as safe haven and home for the banned members of the Bhutanese royal family blends in with the other cream-colored houses on the New Delhi street. Inside, however, the golden brilliance of the chapel and its large statue of the Buddha radiates as the heart of the home. Paintings, statuary and butter lamps surround the Buddha. Next door is a studio where a Tibetan artist creates an elaborate sacred Buddhist painting, called a *thangka*, with rich, vibrant colors. The exiled queen, a friend of the Dalai Lama, frequently hosts Tibetan monks in her home. Walking into the living room and dining room, I see glass-covered cabinets holding vessels and trophies from the royal life in Bhutan.

I climb a flight of steps to the second floor of the princes' home and arrive at an open hall, which is used as a sitting room. What catches my eye immediately are two large framed photographs of the princes as young boys—I recognize each distinctly—dressed in the native attire of Bhutan. The Bhutanese photographer had caught them in boyish moments, one walking down a dirt path, the other looking up into trees. There is a wistfulness about the pictures that seems to embody the longing that is a palpable presence in the house.

I am introduced to the queen, a woman who looks more like a retired movie star than the wife of a Himalayan monarch. She is lounging in a large chair in the sitting area, drinking tea with a friend. She cocks her head to the side when she hears my name, smiles broadly and says clearly, "Hello." Then she turns back to her partner in conversation, says a few words in Bhutanese and lifts a cigarette to her lips.

I am shown to a lovely, airy room with a balcony that overlooks a garden of trees. The room belongs to the youngest princess in the family, now living in California, and I am told to use it as my own. There is no key to this bedroom door. I lie down on the green silk quilt covering the large bed and smile to myself. I am finally here, in India, the land I have dreamt about since I was a small girl.

I am unpacking my clothes after a brief rest, when my bedroom door swings open and Deachen, the eldest sister, introduces herself and enters with the true grace of a princess. She is wearing a body-clinging lavender dress, which she says she knit herself. She takes my hands gently into her own and holds them, all the while giving me a soul-searching look. In her dark eyes I see a melancholy, a longing, that has to be akin to the deep love of homeland I first saw in her elder brother some fifteen years before.

Deachen rubs her hand slowly down the sleeve of my colorful sweater, admiring its texture, and asks me when I was in Tibet. I am surprised at the question, but when she tells me my sweater was hand knit in Tibet, I understand. I explain to her I bought the sweater from a catalog in the United States, where it was advertised as "made in China." She frowns and, shaking her head, says, "No. Someone in Tibet knit this sweater."

Tea is served on a tray, and Deachen pours out the steaming brown brew into white cups. The two of us sit by the open window, enjoying the flavor of the rich Darjeeling tea. As we talk, I hear a corresponding chatter outside among the birds in the trees. Their song seems to be expressing a simple joy. This delicately beautiful woman with sad eyes is telling me a different story—one of yearning for the land of her childhood, the land of her birth. She has had to raise her two children in exile, in a foreign culture. She symbolizes for me the millions of displaced, homeless and exiled people all over the world—people who long for their homeland, their cultural base, the ground that is familiar to them. In contrast, I am able to move about the globe, exploring on my own, and I have my home to return to. I'm one of the lucky ones. In the afternoon sunlight, Deachen and I continue to talk with the greatest ease, as if we were resuming a friendship from somewhere far away and long ago.

It comes as a surprise to me that the princes have never visited the main attractions of New Delhi, so Namgay and his friend Sharon and I set out to sightsee together. We begin in the morning by heading for the very old, and plan to work our way up through the centuries to the new. When we arrive at the red sandstone gate of the Qutab Minar (Qutab's tower) complex south of Delhi, Namgay, tall and athletic with a commanding presence, engages the first guide of many who approach our party.

I learn that Delhi is the site of eight cities, dating back some three thousand years. The Qutab Minar is a soaring, slightly tilting tower five stories high, each story marked with a balcony. It was built to celebrate the change in rule when Muslims from the West conquered the last Hindu kingdom of Delhi and established the Delhi Sultanate, which eventually led to the Moghul Empire. I am looking at the first Muslim structure in India, begun in 1193.

Having spent the previous weeks of my journey surrounded by Christian, and then Hindu and Buddhist architecture, I am curious about the Muslim influence in northwest India and am amazed to see the vast scale and the distinctive Muslim relief work, arches and domes that set these structures apart. The huge Minar towers over everything around it. Nearby is the Might of Islam Mosque, the first mosque built in India, also begun in 1193, by Qutab-ud-din, the Muslim Afghan leader. The mosque stands on top of the foundations of a Hindu temple and is said to be built of materials from twenty-seven idolatrous temples—yet another example of the historical pattern of one civilization conquering and destroying another. The Western notion of progress does not apply here. Rather, I am reminded of the Hindu god Shiva, the destroyer, whose creation rises from the ashes of destruction. I think, too, of new shoots that rise from the debris of the forest floor, of the ongoing cycle of birth and death in nature, but can't reconcile this with the destruction of one civilization by another.

We three wander languidly over dirt paths, an end-of-the-second-millennium exhaust-fume haze hovering over remnants of past glory. Facts cascade over us as our guide spouts the dimensions of the structures, the dates they were built and the rulers who built them. With too much to absorb in too little time, we stop in the muted sunshine to watch school children in navy uniforms play—a flurry of excited little people, who will eventually have their own turn in history.

Sweeping back to town, we head east out Lodi Road to Humayun's Tomb, built in the mid-1500s by the senior wife of the second Moghul emperor, Humayun. Bearing strong Persian influence, the complex structure with its elegant façade, two towers, an archway and a heavy dome, is considered a precursor to the Taj Mahal. This tomb symbolizes a wife's love for her deceased husband, whereas the Taj Mahal declares the love of a husband for his deceased wife. Standing in the late afternoon haze, a weak yellow glow hanging in the sky beyond the trees, I contemplate what a romantic gesture it was to build this imposing, elaborate monument, surrounded by peaceful gardens, to the beloved. It is a gesture I have not seen in the architecture of the Hindu, Buddhist and Christian worlds.

We three close our day of touring by reentering the modern world of New Delhi at Dilli Haat, a large fairground in the south of town. Leaving the contemplative gardens of tombs behind, we join the sights, sounds and smells of living commerce at the All-India Craft Show, where master craftspeople from every state have set up booths to display their artifacts. I'm jostled by people of all ages as we walk among displays of fabrics in warm, sensual tones, woodcarvings of the most intricate sort, fine miniature paintings, luxurious carpets, furniture, clothing—all handmade. Above the crowd floats the pungent aroma of the Indian open-air equivalent of a food court.

I select a few things to buy, and Namgay steps in to negotiate prices for me. It is the thing to do. My Asian hosts cannot tolerate seeing me, a white woman, taken advantage of in a purchasing transaction, so they step in and haggle, making sure I pay the Asian price, not the white tourist's price. Namgay bargains successfully for a small carved elephant of sandalwood, the body a latticework that reveals a baby elephant inside; and for a grain of rice inscribed with my daughter's name, Ellen, and encased in plastic in such a way that the inscription is magnified. I also buy a set of three miniature paintings of female musicians, portrayed gracefully in pastel colors. Each painting depicts a musician playing a different instrument in a garden to an audience of attentive goats or peacocks. When I ask the story of the paintings, the master tells me, through Namgay as interpreter, that they are the work of his best students, that if I were buying a masterwork of his, I would have to pay many thousands of rupees. I am not deterred and take my three miniatures happily.

We end the evening at the food booths, sampling delectable dishes from various states, all served in bowls made of sal leaves, the same leaves I had seen being made into disposable bowls and plates in open-air markets in Nepal. I talk to Namgay about buying some of the leaf plates and bowls, but they aren't for sale here. The next day I find a stack of each on a shelf in my bedroom, ready for me to pack and take home.

I have just finished my morning wash in the antiquated bathroom. The tank over the toilet is so rusted that the water drips on me as I use it, the water heater over the tub so inefficient that the water never gets hot, yet I feel wonderfully refreshed. I am buttoning my dress, when there is a short knock on my bedroom door followed by the entrance of a happy crowd. Jurme, the elder prince, has returned from a trip to Darjeeling, and he is accompanied by his two high-spirited sons, his smiling wife and bubbly little daughter, held in her mother's arms. Deachen, the princess whose company I had enjoyed the day before, follows, wearing another lovely hand-knit dress. Greetings are exchanged all around—I haven't seen Jurme since he left my university twelve years ago, and I'm glad to know that, despite his heavier adult build, he still retains his puckish smile. A plan is made for the day, and within the hour we pile into Jurme's car, leaving the children with the older women in the household, and head out for another day of seeing the town.

We arrive midmorning at the India Gate, the monument bearing the names of eighty-five thousand Indian Army soldiers who died in conflicts at the beginning of the century. The arch stands at the end of Rajpath, or King's Way. Before walking up to the gate itself, Jurme turns to point out the expansive view up the Rajpath to the buildings of the Secretariat and the president's residence on Raisina

Hill. "This is where millions of Indians come each January to watch the huge parade in celebration of their independence from the British," Jurme says. He starts to point but then he stops in confusion. He looks again, and then, sure of his direction, realizes the huge government buildings are obscured by what he calls "morning fog." His Indian wife, Aienla, differs and says the "fog" is actually air pollution. I think it must be part of the same sludge-gray haze I saw hulking over the city when I arrived by plane. In the last decade the air pollution in New Delhi, which now ranks among the worst polluters in the world, has become so bad that the view up this grand avenue has disappeared.

Jurme's gesture, his sweep of the arm toward the hidden expanse of the boulevard, makes me see him once again as the young student beginning his undergraduate studies at Western Carolina University. Jurme was the same age as my son, Peter, and the two grew to be friends. Jurme was already expert at Bhutan's national sport of archery, and one of his early requests after arriving in North Carolina was to find a store that sold arrows. Peter would join Jurme for his archery practice on the university's golf driving range and return home awestruck, having watched him hit the bull's eye of the target from several hundred yards away. "Jurme aims his arrow into the sky," Peter would say, trying to figure out how the young prince knew where to point his arrow to place it with such perfection.

I begin walking the path toward the India Gate. It is a gauntlet of peddlers poised to snare me to buy their wares. I hear the sounds of a flute and turn to catch sight of a turbaned snake charmer crouched on the ground, wooing a cobra, which is bobbing in a rhythmic dance. I walk over to have a closer look. "No bite, no poison, madam," the charmer says, his eyes glinting as he speaks, the cobra continuing to weave its magic. I raise my camera to take a photo of the smiling charmer, the obliging cobra.

The minute the shutter clicks, the charmer's expression becomes calculating and his chant turns to a crisp, "Ten rupees for picture, madam." I am startled by the change, for never in Nepal had someone demanded money from me so crassly. I begin to reach for my change purse when Jurme takes me by the arm and leads me back to his car. "No need to pay money," he says. Following close on our heels is the snake charmer in hot pursuit. "Picture ten rupees, madam," he keeps repeating. Aienla and Deachen dodge discretely into the back seat of the car, and I jump into the front passenger seat and slam the door shut. As I turn to look out the window, the snake charmer bangs angrily on the glass, shouting and hissing his demand for money. I wonder if he is going to sic the snake on me. Jurme throws the car in gear, and like Bond, 007, he speeds away into the morning traffic, leaving the dancing cobra and irate charmer behind.

For the first time on my trip, I feel like the alien that I am. I remember, then, what an older Nepalese man had expressed succinctly one day as the two of us were walking together through the narrow streets of the venerable old town of Bhaktapur.

"The Indians had to fight the British for several centuries," he said, leading me past an old Malla palace. "They feel aggressive and angry toward the white man. The Nepalese did not see a white man until 1951. They find them curious, but do not have a history of subjugation by them."

The snake charmer's insistent demand for payment rings in my ears. My fair skin, silver hair and Western dress serve to announce that I am a foreigner, a "rich" white woman, a ready target. I am suddenly conscious of my race, of being an outsider, and I don't like the feeling. I realize I am a member of the race that did indeed subjugate the Indian people for centuries. I wonder why I didn't give the snake charmer the ten rupees after all. The incident makes me feel empathy for my exiled Bhutanese hosts, who, in India, have been the recipients of violent acts of racial prejudice. If only the differences between peoples were not seen as barriers, but as a diversity to be celebrated!

Before I left home, I had been warned that if I gave so much as a single rupee to one Indian beggar, I would soon have an army of beggars following me. I had been advised by an Asian friend to carry pepper spray in my purse to ward off pursuers. This suggestion had been countermanded by Akum, my first Indian student in North Carolina, who told me I would be better off to use common sense and throw away the pepper spray. His simple rules for a Western woman traveling alone in India: never go out alone after dark; know the safe areas of the cities, and stay within them; when pursued by beggars and peddlers, duck into the nearest shop, and the shopkeeper will chase them away. I took Akum's advice and left the pepper spray at home. I have not regretted it, but the snake charmer's hissing voice stays with me.

As if to divert my attention to more pleasant things, Jurme goes out of his way to find the Bhutan Embassy and proudly shows it to me. He swings past the monument to Mahatma Gandhi, a statue of a spindly man leading a group of followers, commemorating the resistance leader's famous 1930 protest march to extract salt from the sea. When I was a child, old enough to understand the news broadcasts on the radio, I remember praying for that spindly man, that he would not come to harm in his heroic campaign of passive resistance to lift the oppressive yoke of the British from his people.

At the suggestion of Jurme's wife, Aienla, we drive to what was once the private residence of Prime Minister Indira Gandhi, which now is a museum in her honor. Again, I am surprised to learn that Jurme and his sister Deachen have never visited the museum, especially since it was Indira Gandhi who offered protection to their family when they were exiled from Bhutan. Aienla, who has been here before, chides them good-naturedly and leads us to the entrance.

Inside, we are greeted by display cases full of worldwide press coverage of Indira Gandhi's life. We walk past her study and library, kept as they were at the time of her death. We solemnly pass the blood-stained sari Mrs. Gandhi was wearing when her Sikh bodyguards assassinated her on the garden path. But underneath all the public history, I hear the private commentary of Jurme and Deachan, brother and sister, as they point out their father, the king of Bhutan ("Daddy," with the accent on the second syllable), in photographs with the Indian prime minister. They smile knowingly at each other when they see objects throughout the house that their father had given Indira Gandhi as gifts—a bowl here, a plate there, a piece of cloth that they recognize. Jurme is especially impressed by the simplicity of the prime minister's home, remarking that Mrs. Gandhi did not live like the corrupt politicians of the present, "who demand marble for everything." I can't help wondering how my hosts would have spent their lives, if circumstances had been different, as royals in Bhutan.

Our little band of tourists joins Namgay at the Chinese restaurant he manages, and we settle down for a hearty meal. When I comment that the excellent noodle soup is like nothing I have had in a Chinese restaurant before, Namgay tells me that it has been modified for the Punjab taste. I eat my fill of delicious specialties of the house and talk with Deachen about her family and home away from Delhi in a hill station to the east. After the meal, I leave Jurme, Aienla and Deachen behind, and set off with Namgay and Sharon to see yet another site they have never visited: the Lotus Temple.

The urban pollution has thickened the air to a dirty haze, obscuring the clarity of the temple's brilliant design. I can just make out the shape of a giant flower and think that if this were a real lotus, it would be struggling to breathe. The long approach to the temple is filled with hundreds of people, perhaps thousands, streaming in two directions, coming and going, and we join the flow moving toward the stationary flower. As is customary at temples here, we take off our shoes and leave them in bags with men who hurriedly stash them out of sight. I like my walking shoes and wonder if, in this huge crowd, I will ever see them again. In stockinged feet we inch toward the temple.

Completed in 1986 as the Baha'i House of Worship, the graceful building rises to a peak in the shape of the sacred lotus blossom, the flower whose name is on the tongue of millions as they chant the holy mantra, "Hail! The Jewel in the Heart of the Lotus! Hum!" Nine petals rest in a perpetual state of unfolding above pools of cool water. We climb the steps and circle the pools. We walk in silence into the circular interior, into a high, open space filled with long rows of wooden chairs. We walk separately, admiring the beauty in our own ways, stopping to sit and absorb the serenity of the scene.

Imagine being inside a lotus blossom, the jewel in the lotus, the sacred flower that has appeared in the scriptures of the East for thousands of years. The lotus is akin to the water lily, a pastel flower that rises from ponds and lakes in regal posture above large, round, deep-green leaves that hold one silver drop of rainwater in their center. Imagine being inside the palest pastel, swathed in the softest, smoothest petals you have ever felt. Imagine the silence and the peace.

Bahaism is a relatively recent religion the essence of which is the unity of all religions, with the goals of world peace, universal education, and equal respect for women and men. The doors of the temple are open to people of all faiths to worship and meditate in their own ways. The Lotus Temple translates these beliefs to perfection, using the symbol of the lotus flower, thus bringing us back to the ideal of harmony found in nature.

Loving the silence and not wanting to leave, we reluctantly rise and move out onto the open terrace. Namgay gathers literature about the scheduled services, saying he may return some day. I continue walking, circling the pools, enjoying the sensation of polished stone on my stockinged feet. I rejoin the others, and slowly we walk down the steps, falling in line with those who are leaving. I hand a strange man a ticket, and with a deft gesture he gives me my shoes.

Tired but happy from a day of touring, we arrive home at dusk and are greeted with broad smiles from various loyal members of the royal household. I slowly ascend the stairs to my room. When I reach the second floor, I am surprised to find the wooden door to my bedroom open and the curtained glass doors leading to the balcony flung wide. Outside on the balcony wall I see the flames of butter lamps flickering, as sundown stirs the air.

I watch an old man, bent over in humble posture, tending the lamps. He looks up at me with a sweet, toothless smile. I ask Namgay what is happening, and he answers simply, "It is a Buddhist holy day." I contemplate the old man, his face a picture of devotion, as he keeps vigil over the flames of his enduring faith. His body and mind are enraptured in peace. My gaze is drawn to the garden beyond, alight with more lamps, and I stay to admire the quiet evening scene.

Amidst this calm, I feel a motion of impatience, as if a wind has come, threatening to extinguish the flames. I look up at the handsome young prince, who watches the old lamp tender briefly, and I see questioning in his eyes. No patient burning of lamps has helped him achieve his one true desire—to return to his homeland. No earthly reward has come for his family's Buddhist faith. Then, with an impulsive move that feels to me both defiant and resigned, Namgay turns his back and, without a word, is gone.

Jodhpur
Land of Warrior Kings

The eighth wonder of the world!

—Jackie Kennedy,
Entrance Ticket to Meherangarh Fort

It feels anachronistic to arrive in a flying machine in the land of kings. I drop out of the sky into the city of Jodhpur in the midst of Rajasthan, the colorful, exotic state in northwest India that borders Pakistan.

I am traveling with my good friend Rani Aldis and her ever-adaptable ten-year-old son, Ravi. Though Rani and I have known each other in North Carolina for more than twenty years and I have watched her son grow up, here in India we make a strange trio. Rani is a beautiful, dark-skinned Tamil woman, Malaysian by birth, whose family roots are in Sri Lanka, but who now is an American citizen. Her son, a bright boy who loves to read, is lighter-skinned than his mother, revealing the heritage of his white American father. I am the palest, oldest and, in this setting, most foreign-looking of the three.

I soon learn that everyone we meet—hotel clerks, waiters, ricksha drivers, tradesmen in the market—is insatiably curious about our little trio. Not only are we a mixed bag racially, but we are two women traveling without adult male escorts. Why are we traveling together? What is our relationship? And, most important, who is the mother of Ravi?

Rani's husband, William, works for the United Nations, and the family has lived in Africa and Asia for six years; as a result of their peripatetic lifestyle they have developed a private routine for instantly turning a strange place into a home of their own. When I find myself sitting in a room at an outlandish Quality Inn at the edge of the exotic city of Jodhpur with a ten-year-old watching a blaring TV while his mother takes charge of the room, I feel more like the hypotenuse of an isosceles triangle than a happy tourist traveling with an old friend.

I can tell that Rani is as restless as I am. We are both disappointed in the hotel booked for us by a travel agency in New Delhi—it feels like an American motel. I suspect the Indian travel agent thought this is what American women would want, but we had a local sort of place in mind. Suddenly Rani decides to lock her son in the room with the TV, where he will be safe, and she and I walk out into the night to get a taste of the town.

Outside the hotel a line of auto rickshas waits for tourists like us to emerge. Rani approaches the drivers alone and, using a patois of Hindi and English, bargains for the cheapest price to town and engages the driver for the evening. Within minutes I am being conveyed through the night streets of Jodhpur in a small, noisy, three-wheeled auto ricksha. I feel as if I'm in an open cockpit and pull my Nepalese shawl over my nose and mouth to block the cool, polluted air streaming past my face. I cough and ask Rani if she is bothered by the diesel exhaust and foul air. She says, matter-of-factly, "You get used to it."

"Swarm" is the first word that comes to my mind, as we step from the auto ricksha into the dirty city street. Swarms of people are milling past stalls of every description, and the rich aroma of cardamom and turmeric floats from open-air restaurants out into the street. We fall in with the crowd moving along the edge of the thoroughfare, passing numerous shops along the way. Loudspeakers posted at intervals blare a stream of language I cannot understand. We approach the focal point of the Clock Tower and find a huge crowd of soldiers, dark men in dark uniforms, talking and shouting and strutting their stuff. I instinctively pull back, wondering if we, two foreign women, aren't out of our element in this night melee of men. Then I notice the banners and realize we have landed in the midst of a political rally—the national elections are only days away. We pause to watch the shouting, and I wonder if these are some of the men sent out to rally votes for Sonja Gandhi, Rajiv Gandhi's Italian widow, who is seeking control of the Indian Congress Party.

We return to the shops on the street, moving away from the shouting soldiers. I watch older men in colorful turbans, smoking and drinking and talking. They remind me of the men I saw in Greek sidewalk cafés many years ago in my student travels. Rani points out a woman who is wearing a sari draped in the local fashion. Bolts of colorful cloth are for sale, pots and pans, bicycles, gaudy trinkets—all sorts of trade transactions are going on around us. I watch Rani, an experienced world traveler, sizing up the place, her keen eyes taking in the scene. She throws back her head, like a stallion sniffing the wind before a race, and gives a sigh of approval.

I have stepped into an outpost leaning toward the Middle East. Jodhpur has a completely different feel from anywhere I've been so far on this trip—more like a pioneer town out West. Its spirit is rough and ready, its people a hardy bunch of rugged desert dwellers. Rani and I stop in an open-air restaurant for a drink and snack and watch the tide of people moving through the streets ablaze with electric lights under the black sky.

Even from these few hours, I feel how different staying in hotels as a foreign tourist is from the hospitable home stays I have had in Nepal and New Delhi. On the road I take all my impressions from public life—my interactions with people are all of a commercial nature rather than the warm interplay of family life with natives. Sitting at the grimy table watching flies stop to drink from drops of my sweet orange drink, I realize how tired I am. The noise from the loudspeakers grates on my nerves, and I am more than ready to call it a night. We pay a few rupees for our refreshment, locate our driver, who is patiently waiting for us in a crowd of motorbikes and rickshas, and climb in behind him onto the small, open-air seat.

Riding the considerable distance back to our American-style hotel on the edge of town, the cool night wind searing our cheeks, Rani and I resolve to get out of our sterile, expensive lodgings the next day and move to a cheaper local establishment in town. When we arrive in front of our hotel, Rani wants to pay for the ricksha herself, saying she can get the better price if I, a white foreigner, am not involved. As I walk up the steps to the hotel alone, I look back and catch a glimpse of the disgruntled face of our ricksha driver as Rani pays him exactly what she thinks the ride is worth and not a rupee more. Seeing my old friend in this new setting, I find qualities in her I didn't know she had: Rani drives a tough bargain, and she has a mind of her own.

The Clock Tower and Sardar Bazaar in the center of Jodhpur have an altogether different look by day. Sunlight streams down on countless market stalls filled to overflowing with foods and textiles and tools and crafts of every description. Beyond all this, my eye is drawn to an amazing sight—the immense Meherangarh Fort, which rises majestically above the desert city, high on a hill to the northwest. I'm told it is the most formidable fort in all of Rajasthan. Rich in the heritage of chivalrous maharajas (great kings), who once reigned proudly over their own states, this arid land still supports the immense forts and palaces of past centuries, while proffering the commerce of today in crowded streets and hustling markets.

I spend the morning enjoying the lively trade in the bazaar surrounding the Clock Tower. Rani, Ravi and I get an overview of the area by taking a ride in a rickety horse-drawn cart with a pleasant old man, whom Rani takes a liking to. He steers his bony horse through the narrow alleys of the old city, allowing us a leisurely chance to see how the people live. I snap a picture of Rani, looking smart in her white *salwar kameez*—the traditional tunic over loose trousers—holding on to the cart wheel and standing happily next to the old man.

I wander in the open air, content to be swallowed up in the confusion of the market. I gravitate to a used bookstall filled with thousands of paperbacks and pamphlets, some in English. I rummage through boxes and find local maps and a few worn brochures describing the town. I view these tattered souvenirs as treasures— smudged brochures bearing quaint descriptions of the town forty years ago, old maps showing the topography of the area. I'm always looking for the overview, a way to understand how things fit together.

A map can speak thousands of words and take you in your imagination anywhere you want to go. During the years when I was moored at home, with my children still in school, I satisfied my yen for travel by working in my university's map library. For thirteen years I worked with Anita Oser, a superior map librarian, organizing maps that came from all over the world—we even had maps of the heavens and the ocean floors and an atlas of fantasy! It is a great loss that young Americans today have such scant knowledge of geography. Most are not even curious about their local terrain, let alone the rest of the planet. The American indifference to geography reflects our modern urban culture's disregard for the natural world and lack of understanding for our fellow species' habitats.

I move through the crowded bookstall aisles to the old cash register and hand my money for the items I've chosen to a large woman who gives the impression she has seen a lot of hard living. Unabashed, she looks me over and peers quizzically into my bag.

Back in the center of the bazaar, our trio is approached by a young man, probably in his twenties, who offers, in excellent English, to show us the "best places." It is a common practice for locals, called "touts"—whether on foot or driving a ricksha or taxi—to find tourists and take them to shops, restaurants and hotels, where they receive a commission on whatever their victims buy. Unsuspecting tourists can easily be duped by shopkeepers and hotel clerks in league with the touts, but for some reason Rani trusts this man, so we set out together, following him across the market.

He leads us to a craft cooperative where, he tells us, the work of women and men in eighteen surrounding villages is for sale. The building is extensive, several floors high, and we take our time enjoying the handwork of the clothes, wall hangings, jewelry and wood carvings for sale. Rani bargains for me when I find a striking reversible jacket with wood-block printing on the inside and vivid red wool weaving on the outside. She continues to haggle until she gets the lowest possible price, and for this I am grateful, but I am also concerned that the craftspeople who made the clothing in the villages receive fair pay for their expert work. With so many middlemen, I wonder if that is possible.

Out in the streets again, we walk past stalls of fruit, grains, beans and rice heaped in colorful pyramids. We stop to buy saffron from a spice seller; Rani buys a sack of oats for making a traditional porridge. When I find a stall selling brooms, I pause to purchase one, and the broom-maker looks perplexed. Rani reminds me that in India a broom is used by the lowest caste of people, who sweep the streets and floors, and that the broom is also a symbol for getting rid of something or someone you don't like. It is considered an insult to sweep your floor too soon after a guest has left your home. I persist, overcoming the broom-maker's wariness of an American tourist, and find a good-looking broom, hand-fashioned from local reeds. I want it as a gift from India, like the broom of elephant grass I bought in Nepal.

Moving away from Rani and Ravi, I find a smiling young woman, sitting on the cobblestone square, holding an infant. She is wearing a red sari and selling plastic bangles. I buy a set from her, communicating through sign language to figure out the price. The woman looks radiant, and I gesture to ask if I may take her picture. "America?" she asks me, and when I nod yes, she mimes a request for an American coin. All I have is a few U.S. stamps bearing an illustration of a blue jay, and I give them to her. She beams and shows the stamps to her baby. When Rani joins me, she looks askance at the price I have paid for the bangles and that I have given away stamps, to boot. But I have to deal with the people on my own terms and am pleased with my simple purchase and the pleasant transaction with the mother and child. I feel uncomfortable with the hard bargaining over a few rupees—mere cents—that I see is so natural for Rani.

The Meherangarh (Majestic) Fort is an amazing introduction to the forts of Rajasthan. Like medieval fortresses of Europe, it occupies a large area in a strategic location and dominates the local landscape. I am reminded of Edinburgh Castle, also built upon a rock, also consisting of many separate palaces and halls built over centuries.

Our old bus, full of Indian tourists, winds its way slowly up the sandy hill past a series of seven gates, each of which has served to deter enemies in times past, and some of which celebrate military victories. Beside the Loha Pol (Iron Gate), I see small handprints covered in vermilion powder and learn they were made by Maharaja

Man Singh's widows, who, in 1843, threw themselves upon their king's funeral pyre. This ancient ritual of self-immolation, or *sati*, I am told, was part of the chivalrous act of *jauhar*: historically, the proud warriors of Rajasthan would don saffron robes and ride out to greet certain death in battle rather than be defeated by the overwhelmingly huge armies of the ever-expanding Moghul Empire. Seeing the frail handprints gives me a shiver. I contemplate the range of emotions of a proud-hearted, passionate people whose love of their way of life was so intense that they created rituals for sacrificial death rather than live in defeat. What independence, devotion, exaltation and terror they must have known. Those fragile women's handprints signify for me the divergence between my path as a pacifist and their path as wives of warriors.

At the entrance to the fort, I choose to hire a guide to lead me through the vast chambers and levels of the sprawling structure, while Rani and Ravi run off to explore on their own. I pay the extra fee to be allowed to take my camera inside. I look at my large ticket, the size of a postcard, and see Jackie Kennedy's enthusiastic quote: "The eighth wonder of the world!"

My guide is a young student of history, and together we climb to the highest level, then walk out on the ramparts to see an expansive view of the town and Thar (Indian) Desert beyond. The oval shape of the wall defining the old city is discernible, and it is easy to distinguish the houses painted a lavender blue from those that have been whitewashed and resemble the color of the sands on which the town is built. My guide tells me that the blue houses are owned by the Brahmins, or priestly caste of Hindus, but another interpretation suggests that the blue comes from copper sulfate added to the whitewash to deter termites. The blue houses are mainly around the base of the fort because the termite infestation is the greatest there where, coincidentally, many Brahmin families live.

All of the maharajas of Rajasthan, kings of the regional warrior clans, lost their power when the states merged into the Union of India in 1949. Many of the former rulers have stayed in their ancestral homes and converted them to hotels or opened their forts and palaces as museums to attract the tourist trade. This huge fort, begun in 1459, was the stronghold of the Rathore clan of Marwar for nearly five hundred years. It has grown through centuries of battles and expansions to its present size, and is run today by the former maharaja of Jodhpur.

I am glad I have a guide to lead me through the labyrinth of palaces, apartments and armories. He tells me the stories associated with the elaborately decorated royal haudahs, the palanquins, the elegant costumes, fine miniature paintings, folk musical instruments, furniture, including a roomful of cradles, and weapons. I prefer the cradles to the weapons. Not a student of weaponry, I am amazed at the ingenuity and skill needed to forge the large variety of instruments designed to subdue and kill people. Antique guns, shields of rhinoceros hide, iron maces, elaborately designed daggers and huge ornamented swords fill the cases of the armory. There are even swords said to have been used by Tamerlane, the fierce, warring ancestor of the Moghuls, who sacked Delhi in 1398 and reigned from his capital in Samarkand.

Seeing all this reminds me of my terror when, as a student traveling in Germany, I visited a medieval dungeon for the first time. It was filled with instruments of torture designed to extract confessions and information from religious, political and military dissidents. I could not sleep well for weeks afterward, my mind in turmoil, thinking of the victims' suffering.

Leaving the weapons museum, my guide and I move out to discover the many individual palaces built through the centuries for the ruling maharajas. They have irresistibly charming names: Pearl

Palace, Sun Palace, Sleeping Palace, Mirror Palace, Flower Palace. I am fascinated with the Palace of Glimpses, called the Jhanki Mahal, where the maharajas' wives and concubines lived behind intricately carved sandstone *jalis* (latticed windows).The jalis overlook a courtyard and once provided a vantage point for the women to peek through the small openings in the carved designs without being seen. I am shown a hall where the maharaja entertained his women—a large sumptuous pillow rests on the floor under elaborate ceiling decorations of mirrors and paintings.

I wonder how the women in the royal household were instructed in giving pleasure to their king, and I think of the recent powerful film *Kama Sutra,* directed by Mira Nair, a story of love and entanglement in sixteenth-century Hindustan. It is derived from the Indian classic, the *Kama Sutra,* translated as "lessons in love." Roughly sixteen hundred years ago, Vatsayana, a Hindu Brahmin and religious scholar, compiled and summarized the precepts *(sutra)* of love and marriage that had been passed along for centuries. The *Kama Sutra* is one of three fundamental texts that address the necessities of human society as understood in ancient India: the first discusses material goods to ensure survival *(artha);* the second describes erotic practice to ensure transmission of life *(kama);* the third defines rules of behavior to ensure the duration of the species *(dharma).*

I found the film a lavishly sensual portrayal of the traditional Indian art of love, told sensitively from the woman's point of view. Reaching far beyond the common Western reduction of the *Kama Sutra* to a sex manual, the film portrays the high art of love as exquisite sensual communication between the sexes. Nair has pointed out that it is amazing that people in this region of the world could have created so much style around the art of pleasure while the austerity of Puritanism reigned elsewhere. Standing here in the Palace of Glimpses in Meherangarh Fort, I wish I could glimpse that life of pleasure that once reigned supreme in these palace walls.

I round a bend in the massive stone walls of the fort and come upon two colorfully turbaned musicians, a flutist and a drummer, who perform as I walk past. Another anachronism, it seems, to be listening to these tribal musicians of Rajasthan, piping a tune for me, a Western tourist. I know they are hoping for a tip. I hear the piping and drumming as an echo of the music of their ancestors, royal court musicians, who played for the banquets of their victorious kings. Perhaps they spun tunes for Kipling during his travels through the exotic Land of the Rajputs.

I leave Meherangarh Fort slowly and reluctantly, lost in thought. I am here in the space, but not in the time of the proud warrior kings. I have strolled through a carefully planned reenactment of a passionate span in history. I have walked among the bones of the past that have stirred my mind and heart, but I have experienced none of the flesh and blood of the warrior clans and their women who once inhabited this place. The fort of today, like a still life painting, is pleasing to behold, yet it leaves me hungry for a taste of the real fruit, the real pleasure and intrigue of its fabled past. For just one moment, I succumb to its lure. I wish I could shed my twentieth-century idealist, pacifist cloak and don instead the silk sari of a striking courtesan and look down through the jalis, waiting to be summoned to the Pearl Palace to lie next to the beating heart of my maharaja.

Jaisalmer
Desert Peacock

My heart is like a singing bird.
—Christina Rossetti, "A Birthday"

The night train to Jaisalmer is packed. I've just made up my bunk bed with a sheet, small pillow and wool blanket on top of a long plastic cushion that makes noise every time I shift position. Rani and Ravi are in the two bunks opposite and an Indian man is in the bunk above me. We are all wearing our street clothes. A large heavy curtain is drawn across the compartment, separating us from the aisle where the conductor and other passengers walk. This is my first encounter with the Indian railway system, and I'm still trying to digest the scene in the station we just left.

I have never seen cows wandering through a train station and onto the boarding platform before. I have never seen a large, central waiting hall carpeted with people, wrapped in blankets, sleeping on the cold stone floor. They were virtually camping out, with water bottles and thermoses of tea and snacks, waiting for trains that were hours late, sometimes six to eight hours late. Even with so many human beings packed next to one another, I observed a separateness, one from the other. There was no talking; the hall was strangely quiet.

I was looking for a place in the hall for the three of us to camp, when Rani steered us to a sign at the far end of the hall that indicated a waiting room for foreigners. Again, I felt singled out as an alien as we stepped over and around the people stretched out on the floor and walked into the small waiting room, past a man acting as sentinel at a makeshift desk. We sat down on upholstered chairs and each bought a little glass cup of milky tea from a vendor and sipped it while we waited. We were in a room full of white Europeans, some with backpacks and hiking boots, all the people much bigger than those sleeping outside on the floor. Ravi was the youngest person, and I was the oldest. The foreigners' waiting room was filled with talk and laughter.

I wondered how Rani and Ravi felt, both looking more akin to those on the floor in the hall than to the Europeans and me. Neither gave indication of anything unusual. Ravi curled up in his chair with a book and paid no attention to the rest of us. Having traveled with his parents since he was a young boy, he is amazingly resilient.

Now we are here, on this train, for the next eight hours, traveling through the night from Jodhpur to Jaisalmer, an old fortified town to the west in the Thar Desert, and once a trading post on the Silk Road. Rani and I are reading by the tiny electric bulbs provided in our bunks, taking advantage of a bit of time and space to ourselves. When I am no longer able to concentrate on someone else's writing, I put down my book and turn off the reading light. I lie in the dark, enjoying the rhythmic shuffle of the old train moving over the tracks.

I feel a sense of anticipation because tomorrow, December 18, is my birthday. I like the idea that I will be in the most remote location of my journey. I like the symbolism of traveling into the desert, away from civilization, to celebrate my sixtieth birthday. My mind scans my past, as it has so often on this trip, this time surveying the birthdays that marked the beginning of each new decade of my life.

Without any special effort, I remember the tenth, twentieth, thirtieth, fortieth, fiftieth, wondering again if my propensity for numbers is related to my fascination with music.

When my parents asked me what present I would like for my tenth birthday, I had no trouble answering: I wanted to eat a whole lobster by myself—I didn't want to share one with my younger sisters. I was surprised when they agreed and took me to eat at Beck's on the Boulevard in Philadelphia. The place was festively decorated for the Christmas holidays, and I sat at the restaurant table surrounded by my family, using the slender fork to pull out each tender morsel from the claws of my very own lobster. I felt happy that I had finally reached the age of double digits. I was secure in my world of family, music and school and was so content with my life I didn't want it to change.

My twentieth birthday I celebrated in Munich, where I was studying music, German literature, art history and philosophy. For my birthday dinner I was treated by my German mentor, Thea Bach, to an elaborate meal that began with a shot of Slivovitz. I ate Rehrücken, saddle of venison, that was as deliciously dark and earthy as my tenth-birthday lobster had been light and of the sea. During that year based in Munich I inhabited a suspended state of ecstasy—I was in Europe on my own, testing myself without family and friends, steeping myself in the cultural life of music, opera, theater, art, cafés, cabaret, and using every spare moment I could find to travel. I was dating German and other European men more than I had ever dated in the United States. I was flying high and did not want the year to end.

On my thirtieth birthday I was living in Appleton, Wisconsin, wife of a professor of German, mother of two children, age two and five months. I was imbued with domesticity, still nursing my daughter, running the household of my family in a traditional way that had more in common with my mother's domestic scene in the thirties, when I was born, than with the pop culture of the late sixties, in which I was living. I was devoting my energy exclusively to the needs of my family and had no time left over for myself. I was gloriously thankful to have a faithful husband and two beautiful children. I don't remember my birthday dinner.

I have a picture of myself on my fortieth birthday, wearing a beige, plaid Pendleton suit, standing in front of the Biltmore House in Asheville, North Carolina. I have other pictures from the same day taken with my husband and son and daughter. I was still a wife and mother and had become active as a community volunteer in Cullowhee, a small university town nestled in a valley below the Blue Ridge Parkway. In the photo I look pleased in a mature sort of way. During the previous decade I had lost both my parents to cancer and heart disease, and I was aware that I had inherited the vanguard position in my birth family. I imagined I would be the next to die.

I think of my fiftieth birthday as one of the dark days of my life. My husband was driving the two of us through Cades Cove, part of the Great Smoky Mountains National Park, and I was trying to communicate with him. I asked him to stop at the old Baptist church so that we could get out of the car and talk. The church was locked. It was bitter cold, the ground was covered with a thin layer of snow, and my feet were freezing. We were estranged, teetering on the brink of divorce. After our two children had gone away to graduate school and college, it had become eminently clear to me that even though we had lived together for twenty-six years, my husband and I had not achieved the close union I longed for. My daily interior monologue was one of pure frustration; my attempts to reach out to my husband, to build an intimate relationship with him, had failed. My later ventures, which I did not actively seek, to enjoy friendships with men beyond the confines of my home had put our marriage in grave jeopardy.

As we walked in the cemetery of that Baptist church in the snow on my fiftieth birthday, all I longed for was positive change. I asked my husband to stop and listen a moment to what I had to say. I told him the best birthday present he could give me would be a fresh start together. But even when he stood still, his eyes were not seeing me, his ears were not hearing; he was gazing instead into the winter woods beyond, lost in a world of his own. My words, a plea to shake us out of the doldrums of depression, to forgive each other for our past hurts and disagreements, fell unheard onto the hard, cold stones. We returned to the car and drove to a cozy restaurant in Gatlinburg for my birthday dinner, but the warmth of the place did nothing to relieve the chill in my heart. I had no desire to eat. I remember driving home through a vast forest of bare trees in cold, dark silence, feeling utterly without hope.

A few years earlier I had promised myself that, when I turned fifty, I would dedicate the year to celebrating myself, a kind of sabbatical for sacrificing many of my own interests—for more than two decades—to the needs of my husband and children. With the realization on my fiftieth birthday that everything I had tried to build with my husband had in fact collapsed, I was confounded. And there was no intimation, no omen that the sadness had only begun. Within twelve weeks I would be confronted with the death of my son.

Lying in the darkness of this Indian railway carriage, I consider how my last decade has been one of hitting rock bottom, then gaining the clarity to know I didn't want to keep living in an abyss of sorrow, and finally taking the necessary steps to rebuild my life.

It took a lot of energy to start over again on my own, but since I thrive on new experience, I also gained energy. And now this solo birthday trip around the world is my reward, my postponed sabbatical gift to myself.

When I place my right foot on the step of the old army jeep and reach to pull myself up into the back seat, I scrape my left shin on metal. It smarts, and I see that the skin is cut, marking me on my sixtieth birthday. Rani jumps into the front seat with the jeep driver, a swarthy, reserved man, and they talk now and then in a mixture of Hindi and English as we leave Jaisalmer and head out into the desert. I sit in the back with Ravi, hair blowing in the dry wind, and when I turn around to look out the rear hatch, I have an uninterrupted view of the empty road behind.

It is a warm, bright day, and I can see across the flat expanse to the horizon. It looks desolate and inhospitable to settlement, but after a while we turn off the main road and drive over a sandy path to Amar Sagar, where once there was a formal garden. The lake is dry this time of year. The noonday sun is hot, and we walk the grounds separately, moving slowly in the heat toward the walls of a Jain temple being restored. Ornate carvings glow in a cream color akin to the shade of the desert sand. The isolation of the place takes me back to the American Mojave Desert, where one day, years ago when I was camping out West with my family, we stopped at a crossroads for gasoline. I was so overwhelmed by the desolation of the spot and the lonely life I imagined for the young Shoshone boy who filled our gas tank that I started to cry and couldn't stop. Walking the grounds of this remote Jain temple in the Thar Desert of Rajasthan, I feel a sense of purposeful seclusion rather than unwilled isolation, and I am not sad here.

Jainism arose around 500 B.C. in the same period as Buddhism. Both religions attempted to lay out new, simpler spiritual paths in response to the dominance and complexities of Hinduism. I admire the Jain belief in *ahimsa*, reverence for all life. Jains are strict vegetarians and avoid all professions that involve harming or killing animals. They are divided into two sects: the white-clad Shvetambara and the sky-clad Digambara, who live naked, showing their disdain for material possessions. I was disappointed earlier when I was refused admittance to a Jain library in Jaisalmer that houses ancient manuscripts I wanted to see, so I enjoy spending time now among the temple carvings of these non-violent believers.

We continue touring, the jeep driver taking us dutifully to see cenotaphs, the remains of villages, a bleak earthen house standing solitary off the road. Early in the afternoon we stop at a soft-drink stand with a few tables, a desert outpost where our driver will receive a commission from anything we buy. I long for a glass of fresh, cold water, but I settle for a sweet, sticky, canned orange soda. The proprietor of the stand, seeing Ravi, tries to sell us candy, but Rani quickly intervenes and then becomes caught in conversation with the man.

The soft-drink vendor takes a measure of Ravi's mixed racial features and tries to decide whether he is my son or Rani's. He asks Rani if he is her son, and she says, "No. He's the son of a friend." Ravi's head is in a book, and he makes no reply, but I know he has heard what his mother has just said. I'm surprised and a little shocked that Rani denied her own son to a stranger.

I watch Rani banter with the soft-drink man, and I begin to see how her allegiances are being pulled in many directions on this trip, a journey I had originally hoped would be just the two of us stepping out together for some carefree fun. Perhaps when talking to this local Rajasthani man, who tells her proudly about his children, she becomes sensitive about having a white husband and tries instead to share an Indian identity with the man. I am thinking now, that I, with my pale skin and naive and clumsy Western ways, must also be an embarrassment to her. Earlier in the day Rani told me that the hotel clerk, speaking with her in her native Tamil tongue, had asked her why she put up with being a nurse to "that rich English lady," meaning me. Rani laughed off the incident, but I can see race has become an issue during our travels in India. It rankles me that we have been reduced by strangers to black and white, when I simply see Rani as a good friend.

We return to the jeep and continue heading west into the Thar Desert. In the distance I see a few figures by the side of the road, and as we approach them I find camels, some standing, some lying down by the road, with their drivers. We dismount the jeep, and then the haggling begins—not by Rani, but between the jeep driver and the camel driver, both raising their voices and shaking their fists. The camels seem unconcerned—they look off into the desert, their lips curled in a perpetual smile.

After what sounds to me like harsh words, it is agreed that Rani, Ravi, and I will each ride our own camel. I am introduced first to my camel, named Peacock—the driver tells me he owns the other two camels and is saving his money to buy Peacock. Then I learn that the driver's name is Abdul.

I concentrate on the business of mounting my camel. While Peacock is lying down, I swing my right leg over his back and settle into the saddle. I hang onto the pommel and lean far back to stay balanced while Peacock first raises his forequarters, then straightens his hind legs, and finally straightens his forelegs to a standing position. I locate the stirrups with my feet and take the reins, which are fastened to the camel's nose peg. I am high in the air and surprisingly comfortable in the saddle.

Ravi is excited and smiling broadly because he does not have to share a camel with his mother. Abdul, wearing a white tunic over a dark sarong, a white cap and pointed leather slippers, tactfully lets Ravi take the lead and walks alongside the camels in the sand. With his limited English, Abdul begins a conversation with Rani on the familiar theme of how we three are related. Then he starts asking questions of me—Am I married? Why not? If I am not married, I must have a big job back in the States to be able to travel to Rajasthan. What is my big job?

I laugh at the idea that my position in the library back home is being described as a "big job." The camel driver thinks I'm rich. He is hoping for a big tip, big enough to help him buy Peacock. Here in India, even riding a camel in the desert, it is important to establish the class distinctions and economic relationships between people.

After an hour, Abdul asks me whether I mind if he rides Peacock with me. I say I don't mind, curious to see what he will do. He mounts the standing camel with the ease of an acrobat climbing a wire and settles behind me. He continues to ask me questions, but I don't think he understands my answers. He talks about his life as a camel driver and suggests I come with him on a four-day camel safari, making a loop around the desert, camping out each evening. Then he dismounts the camel as easily as he had mounted and gently directs Peacock ahead so that I take a turn in the lead. The late afternoon air turns cool, and Abdul drapes a purple cloth over his right shoulder.

We settle into silence. Once again slowed down to the pace of nature, I rejoice in the absence of civilization and the open expanse before me. Surrounded by desert, I feel as if I am visibly inhabiting the unseen time-space inside of me, where any dream is possible and no markers show the way. All I hear is the ringing in my ears and the rhythmic pacing of camel hooves in the sand.

• • •

Evening approaches, and I see tall dunes in the distance. Our camels are heading toward the outpost of Sam, the last settlement before the border with Pakistan. My map shows a few roads leading beyond this point, but they all stop before the border, like so many dead ends. As we near the dunes, I hear distant laughter and talking and look around to see other strings of camels coming from many different directions.

The sun is a ball of fire above the uninterrupted desert horizon. Abdul steers us away from the others to the far end of the dunes, and Peacock steps gracefully through the high sands. We continue on the ridge of the dunes, and then amble to a slightly lower level. When their driver signals a halt, the camels bend their forelegs, then their hind legs, and finally settle their forequarters comfortably in the sand. I dismount carefully and am unsteady at first when I am back on the ground, but after a few steps, I walk easily up the dune.

When I reach the ridge, the previously loquacious camel driver says quietly, as if speaking to the wind, "I must pray," and moves a discreet distance away. I watch him remove the purple scarf from his shoulder and lay it out on the sand, as a prayer rug, facing the setting sun. I am touched by this gesture. During much of the safari Abdul had talked about money and getting rich. He had tried to entice me to stay longer so that he would earn more rupees. But now that we have reached our destination and it is sunset, he leaves all the talk of commerce behind and retreats to a world of prayer. I watch him kneel down, touch his head to the cloth and then return to a sitting position. All the while he is reciting verses from the Qur'an. Think of the centuries of camel drivers who, like this man, have paused in their daily work to bow their bodies and speak these same prayers! Tradition says the prophet Muhammad received the divine word of the Qur'an in the seventh century, and millions of Muslims, worldwide, have been stopping ever since, five times a day, to unfurl their prayer rugs toward Mecca and pray.

I find a place for myself on the dune and sit down, facing the falling sun. In the silence, I listen to my own thoughts. On this my birthday, I think of my mother, from whose body I entered the world. "You have brought the happiness of my lifetime to me" were words she wrote in an old college bluebook to describe my beginnings. A few pages later she went on to record in her lovely, graceful handwriting, "If only there were some way to congeal this ecstasy we find in you now!" Congeal this ecstasy! My mother's narrative was wholly focused on life within the walls of her home and her happiness with her daughter and husband. Her writing was bathed in light; everything she observed radiated with the exuberance of new experience. I, her first-born, had arrived in the dark after sunset on a Sunday evening three days before the winter solstice, on one of the shortest days of the year.

One of the gifts I treasure from my mother is her love of language and literature. She communicated to me, better than any teacher I ever had, the beauty of spoken and written English. I loved to hear her speak, whether she was reciting poetry she had memorized and made her own or reading aloud from the classics because she found them beautiful.

Though my mother was reserved in showing her emotions, I can still feel the hug she gave me at the railroad station as she sent me off to college in Ohio. It was an all-encompassing, never-to-be-forgotten mother's embrace. I remember that heartfelt farewell in contrast to her fragile parting smile at the time of her death. On this, my sixtieth birthday, I am just seven years younger than my mother was when she died.

The orb of fire continues its descent over the Thar Desert. Kneeling in the sand and facing the sun, I close my eyes and see the reverse image of the sunset on my inner eyelids, like a negative of a photograph. Turning to my far left, I see the camel driver still steeped in his evening worship. Like him, I offer a prayer—a prayer of gratitude for my life.

Instantly, another prayer of thanks, said years ago in Germany, comes to mind. Peter was six years old, and I had taken him and Ellen to visit their first cathedral. I had suggested we all say a prayer, and Peter had asked me what a prayer was. "It is a way of talking with God," I had answered, "a way of giving thanks or asking God's help." Both children kneeled in a pew, Ellen watching Peter, and Peter watching me, kneeling under the vaulted arches of the German cathedral. "I told God, 'Thank you for my life,'" Peter said, as we emerged from the church onto the streets of Münster.

From a distance, faint music and the cadences of quiet conversation waft across the dunes. I rest my hands in the warm sand and feel the evening breeze begin to cool my skin. Just as I have traveled across the globe from the lush forests of the Blue Ridge Mountains to the stark beauty of this Indian desert, so have I traversed in this last decade of my life the world of emotion—from deepest sorrow to profound joy. I made the journey, step by step, day by day.

Moving in small increments to achieve an ideal is something at which women excel. Rarely do wives and mothers have large intervals of time to pursue, undistracted, a personal goal. It takes patience, perseverance and determination to stay on track. And it takes vision.

Sitting at sundown with the open horizon before me, I sketch the arc of my life in the sand. It begins with my birth, as celebrated by my mother's unbounded joy, and moves to a first awareness of death at an early age, heightening my appreciation of my life. The

arc continues through a childhood defined by the delight of discovery, not only of my surroundings, but of love as the highest
medium of communication. Developing my talents and moving out
into the greater world, I learn that the diversity of people—and all
forms of life—is to be cherished: the differences between us are
insignificant in light of what we hold in common. Not until I
inhabit the darkness of personal sorrow do I gain some small perspective on my life within the mystery of creation. No matter how
minute I feel in the vastness of time-space, I know clearly that, like
the moth to the flame, I strive toward the light.

The closure of the arc, like the close of my life, remains a question.

Watching the sun disappear, I relish the gift of my life. I am
grateful to those who have shared with me both the wild and the
tender moments. In the golden light of this desert sunset, I give
thanks for all my days.

Udaipur
White on White

Eat and drink until the white thread can be distinguished by you from a black one at the dawn.

—The Qur'an

White is the color of the Jagat Niwas Palace Hotel. In the white courtyard, steep white stone steps that lead up to our room cling to the white wall. A white terrace overlooks the waters of Lake Pichola next to the white covered dining space where I can have a meal or a drink anytime I wish. Our room is up in a corner to itself, an exotic hideaway, including an inviting window alcove with plush, deep-green velvet bolsters where Ravi sleeps. The white marble bath has a shower and toilet paper. And at the entrance to our room, a covered porch with swing looks out over the courtyard and to the lake beyond. Sitting in the swing, I yearn for something exciting to happen.

I'm staying in the old city of Udaipur, the most romantic place I have yet visited on my trip. I feel instantly at home here in an environment that speaks more of beauty than brashness. The narrow streets of the medieval town are as crowded with shops and people as anywhere I've been, yet I don't feel put off by it. I like walking out on my own, memorizing my route through the winding streets, like Hansel dropping bread crumbs along the path, so that I can find my way back to the hotel.

In this poetic town, I long for the company of Thomas, to share the delight of discovery with him. The longer our trio travels together, the more we seem to be going our individual ways. I suspect Rani, too, would rather be here with her husband, William, than with me. It's an intimate kind of place that makes you want to share the day with someone you love.

I move to the hotel roof and bask in the late morning sun. Soft Rajasthani flute music floats up from the restaurant below, and as if in accompaniment, the rhythmic pounding of local women washing their clothes echoes from across the lake. Slap, slap, pound, pound, the women beat the colorful reds and golds on the brown lakeside stone to clean the fabric, and then rinse it in the murky lake, where a few people are swimming. A slow pontoon takes tourists to the Lake Palace Hotel, the former maharaja's palace that floats like a mirage on the water. It is the most extravagant luxury hotel in all of Rajasthan, but I would rather be here than on the island. I like the privacy of the Jagat Niwas and the freedom to come and go as I wish in the old town. Beyond the white hotel wall, monkeys play in the trees, climbing and chattering to themselves. A chipmunk crawls up onto the next table, eats the crystal sugar from the bowl and then, with what must be practiced expertise, knocks over the small metal teapot and crawls inside to drink the dregs.

Only fifteen more days remain of my odyssey, but I feel as if I could keep going indefinitely. I'm in travel mode, and it's a wonderful gear to be in. It's an entirely separate state of mind from that of being rooted in a particular spot. The essence is movement. The challenge is confronting the new. There is no boredom of routine, no daily job to go to, no responsibilities other than to myself.

I'm on my own today. Rani and Ravi have gone off to tour the City Palace, but I feel more like relaxing and ambling the streets. I slowly pull myself away from the luxury of lounging and walk to the main square in town. I enter the cool Kashmir Emporium and stop to admire the richly woven wool rugs. I inquire about one called "The Tree of Life," and the urbane salesman names a price in rupees that is too high for me to calculate into dollars. His appraising eyes suggest he knows I don't have the money to buy a carpet, so he shows me a glass case full of lace, also handmade in the northern state of Kashmir. I buy an intricate white doily for a friend back home. Outside, the midday December sun beats down, and I head for a canvas-covered open-air restaurant on the square. The place is full, and the waiter puts me at a table with a shy, middle-aged Indian couple. I am the only white person, and the woman regards me carefully. The man smiles and quietly says hello. I drink my fresh lime soda in silence, watching the crowd.

Later, walking down the street, I catch sight of a shelf of carved, wooden animals—camel, elephant, horse, bird. The ever-attentive shopkeeper approaches and invites me to have a closer look. He's a thin man in his thirties, well spoken, and I follow him up the rough-hewn wooden steps into his stall. He tells me he is a Brahmin and that he owns a factory on the edge of town where he engages local people to make paper. He shows me his blank books of all sizes. With flowers and leaves strewn throughout the paper, the pages have the freshness of a meadow. The books are sewn with twine and bound in camel skin—I think of Peacock, and then remember camels are used in Rajasthan the way horses and cattle are used in the United States. I can't resist the books and set two aside with the wooden bird and camel.

When the shopkeeper hears that I love books, he takes down an old copy of the epic *Ramayana,* opens the pages to a woodcut and begins reading the Sanskrit aloud. He translates the passages for me, running his finger along the text as he reads. He is so enjoying the story that he asks me, when his cousin enters the stall, if I won't join them for tea, which I do. The cousin pours out the milky tea from a battered metal pot into small ceramic cups, and we drink while my host continues reading.

A while later the shopkeeper mentions his "magic colors" and I ask to see them. He pulls down a series of glass jars filled with stones. In a mortar he crushes the stones individually with a pestle, pounding them into colored powder. After tearing a sheet of white paper into two-inch squares and twisting them into makeshift cups, the shopkeeper sprinkles the colored powders from the various stones into the cups. He adds water from a small pitcher, and voilà! The dyes made from the crushed stones present a rainbow of magic colors different from the colors of the uncrushed stones.

I ask to buy five grams of five colors for an artist friend back home. The shopkeeper carefully sifts each colored powder onto a small rectangle of clear, thin plastic and then measures each little mound on his brass hanging scale. He lights a candle stub with a match and drips wax into the top of one of the glass jars and places the candle in the melted wax until it stands firm, as in a candleholder. He picks up each of the five piles of colored powder, and passing the edge of the folded plastic quickly over the flame, seals each into a tidy pouch. I am delighted by the simplicity of the process. It pleases me to see this man use his ingenuity and skill to make things to order, in contrast to the ready-made goods in prefabricated containers I find back home.

The commotion caused by the stone crushing and the candle flame has attracted a pretty young woman from Bombay wearing a beige salwar kameez that serves as the perfect backdrop for her long, black pigtail. She climbs the steps into the stall and begins asking questions of both me and the shopkeeper. She orders some of the colored powder for her tie-dyeing, and the shopkeeper quickly obliges. I enjoy watching the interaction between the two and notice the woman does not bargain with the shopkeeper harshly, but briefly, in a normal conversational tone.

When I finally move to settle my account, the shopkeeper sees a ballpoint pen in my purse and asks politely if he can have it. I suggest a trade for one of his small blank books, and he happily agrees. I gather my purchases, thank him for the tea and bid him farewell. All this conversation and bartering confirms my impression that successful bargaining can occur in a variety of styles—from the gentle banter of the Bombay woman, to the firm insistence of Rani, to the cutthroat contract of the camel driver. As in my previous forays with local people, I feel pleased that I can deal in my own way with the shopkeeper and that it is a pleasant experience. I head home to my palace hotel, feasting my eyes on all the sights, walking with a light step.

It is the dark of evening. Rani, Ravi and I have just climbed the long stairway to Heaven, a rooftop restaurant, where we are seated in the open air above the town. We each choose something different from the menu. I order a special locally spiced Rajasthani dish, Rani chooses a vegetarian dinner, and Ravi orders his favorite, chicken curry. We will have to wait a while for our meals, which are begun from scratch after the cook receives the orders.

In the streets below there is a lot of animated talk, and I hear what sounds like gunshots. I ask the waiter what is going on, and he replies, "Those are not gunshots. They are firecrackers. People are celebrating the beginning of Ramadan." He points to the pale crescent moon—a sliver of shining white in the black sky, hanging just above the horizon and accompanied by a single bright star—and tells me the new moon indicates the beginning of Ramadan, the holy month of fasting for Muslims.

Rajasthan has a large population of Muslims, and I enjoy learning about their culture. This is the year 1419 by their lunar calendar, which is reckoned from the year of the Hegira, Muhammad's flight from Mecca to Medina. Each new month is determined by sighting the new crescent moon. Ramadan commemorates the month in which the first chapters of the Qur'an were revealed to the prophet Muhammad by the angel Jibreel, or Gabriel, in a cave in Mount Hira. It is a time of fasting and contemplation, a time to show compassion for those less fortunate than oneself.

Islam teaches: "The month of Ramadan may consist of twenty-nine days, so when you see the new moon, observe fast, and when you see the new moon again at the commencement of the month of Shawwal, then break it, and if the sky is cloudy for you, then calculate it and complete thirty days." As for determining what times of day to fast, the Qur'an states: "Eat and drink until the white thread can be distinguished by you from a black one at the dawn. Then fulfill the fast until the night." I watch the new moon and star from the Heaven restaurant, and within half an hour both have set in the West.

By the time our dinners arrive, we are starved. I eat my spicy Rajasthani meal hurriedly because I want to attend a concert at eight o'clock. Nonetheless, we three enjoy the festive atmosphere of firecrackers and fireworks popping and sizzling around us, a last burst of excitement before the month of fasting begins. Then in a quiet moment, we hear singing, men's voices chanting in the distance. The music must be coming from a mosque.

It is a night filled with music. In the afternoon I had stopped in a shop to buy tapes of Indian ragas, and the owners, two brothers who are musicians themselves, asked whether I would like to hear a concert of classical Indian music that evening. When I inquired where the concert was to be held, the answer was, "In a hall. We will take you there." For some reason I trusted the men and accepted their invitation. After dinner I convince Rani to join me and meet the brothers in front of their shop. Ravi declines and goes off to catch a showing of the James Bond thriller *Octopussy,* which was filmed in Udaipur.

The brothers lead us through alleys and dirt paths so narrow and intricate I know I will not be able to find my way back. We pass cows, goats, chickens and dogs along the way. Finally we come to a painted entrance, and the elder brother knocks on the door. Rani asks what kind of building it is, and he answers, "Home."

A woman appears and leads us through a beaded doorway into "the music room," a small space with an alcove displaying a variety of folk instruments. Rani and I are invited to sit in the two bamboo chairs, and the two brothers, joined by an older cousin, sit on cushions placed on mats on the floor. Above them is a colorful poster of Saraswati, the Hindu goddess of wisdom and music, sitting on her vehicle, the white swan, and holding a *vina*, a stringed instrument.

Krishna, the elder brother, begins tuning his tabla hand drums by hammering the little wedges of wood that control the tension of the goatskin surface. Ghopal, the shy younger brother, tunes his sitar, and the cousin warms up on his flute. I watch him closely, because he is playing a six-holed transverse bamboo flute, similar to the teakwood flute I bought a few weeks ago from the wild-haired Gorkha flutist in Pokhara, Nepal.

The sitar player begins stroking his strings, feeling his way into the beginnings of a Kofi raga, a song with a special scale, meant to be sung in the evening. The tabla player gradually joins him on the drums, establishing a complex rhythmic pattern, and the flutist adds his melody. The music is gentle, refined and welcome to my spirit.

Then the flutist, speaking to Rani, explains the words to the next evening raga he will sing, accompanying himself on the harmonium by using his left hand to operate the bellows and his right hand to play the miniature keyboard. He says it is a song about Meera, a woman who has a crush on the god Krishna and waits all night for Krishna to come visit her. Rani smiles and says that Krishna is a playful and mischievous god. The melody of the plaintive song swirls in the air and fills the whitewashed walls of the little music room hidden back in a corner of the old town of Udaipur.

When the playing stops, I want to communicate with the men as a fellow musician. I show them my table of the ten classical Indian thats, or scales, that I copied out and learned when I was visiting Indira in Kathmandu. The flutist looks at the page and says, "Ah, but they are only the fathers. They have many children." It was his way of referring to the numerous variations and combinations of these basic scales that make up the melodic material, the musical families, of the enormous variety of Indian classical ragas that are sung and played. The flutist asks me to sing the scales. I am up for the challenge and begin. He beams as I sing the intervals of the scales correctly. When I reach the eighth Purbi scale, I miss one of the half-step intervals, and he frowns, correcting me with his tenor voice. I continue until I have sung them all. He sees that I am serious and gives me a pat of encouragement on the arm.

It's late, and the cousin and brothers offer to walk us back to the main path. They carry a light and show us the way over tree roots, around a fountain, up a small incline and finally out to the street. Back at the hotel Rani and I climb the steps to the roof terrace overlooking the lake, no longer bright with sun, but cool under the dark sky. Relaxing together at the end of a long day, the distance between us dissolves. We have been friends for such a long time, and in this quiet place with no one else around, no one to see the outward differences between us and ask prying questions as to why we are together, we are able to return to our old, easy friendship. We talk about the things I thought we would discuss traveling together— the future of our lives, our families, our personal goals and desires.

We watch the white lights shimmer across the dark water. All the while we hear the haunting voices of men singing their prayers in the mosque, welcoming Ramadan.

Rani's graceful dark hands are moving over me. She's speaking rapidly, in an uncharacteristically excited way. I am beginning to hear what she is saying. "Oh my God, I thought you were dead!" she exclaims. Rani is kneeling next to me on the cold, white, marble floor of the bathroom. My stomach heaves, and she grabs the red bucket from the shower stall. She helps pull me a few inches off the floor, and I vomit into the bucket and lose every ounce of the specially spiced Rajasthani dinner I ate hours before. I am so weak that I fall back onto the cold, stone floor. My head is pounding, and I'm ice cold. I hear Rani above me.

"Ravi woke me up calling, 'Mama, I heard a tree crash.' I saw a crack of light under the bathroom door and tried to open it, but you had fallen so that your body was blocking the entrance. I pushed and pushed until I was able to budge the door open. And there you were, lying in a big pool of blood! Look at you! Blood everywhere!"

Rani is a nurse, an expert nurse, who has worked in operating rooms and emergency rooms of hospitals and clinics on four continents. When I see her hovering over me, raising my head to wrap a towel around it, I am not the least bit worried. I know I am in excellent hands.

"I couldn't find your pulse. You were as white as a sheet. I thought you were dead!" she repeats. "I said to myself, 'She's just had her sixtieth birthday, and now she's fallen dead of a heart attack. What am I going to do? She's a foreigner. How am I going to dispose of the body? I'll have to contact the American Embassy.'"

I'm lying still on the cold floor, but I'm not bothered by anything

Rani is saying. I reach up to touch the back of my head, which hurts. I feel a clump of sticky, matted hair and a lump on my skull.

"Don't touch that now," Rani says. "You must have hit your head on the wall as you went down, and you have a big gash. I don't know if it will need stitches, but I'm going to put pressure on it."

She reaches for a washcloth, dampens it and wipes the blood off my face. She rolls the cloth together and applies it to my scalp, pressing hard. I shut my eyes again to block out the white light and hear her running water and mopping the blood from the floor with a towel.

"Finally I could feel a faint pulse, and I knew you were alive," she continues. "You must have fainted and fallen backwards onto the floor."

Now I remember. I had an upset stomach during the night and couldn't sleep. I took my first Bromo Seltzer of the trip, feeling the irony of overeating on the eve of the Muslim month of fasting. After I swallowed the tablet, I felt even worse. I went into the bathroom—and then my memory stops.

"We've got to get you back to bed," Rani says. "I'll finish cleaning this up later." Though Rani is a small woman, she is tough and strong. She reaches under my shoulders and gives me the support I need to stagger to my feet. She holds me tight and, with her help, I am able to walk back to my bed. She covers my pillow with towels, trying to keep the damage from the blood to a minimum, and gives me a wet cloth to press against the cut on my head. It's four o'clock in the morning.

Rani's firm hand is reassuring. I know she has saved my life. She says the spicy food was too much for my body, my blood pressure plummeted, and I lost consciousness. I can't imagine how I would have recovered without her.

I shut my eyes and return to the comfort of dark. Despite Rani's initial panic, I feel perfectly calm. It is the same calmness I have felt the few times I've been seriously ill—when I had acute nephritis as a girl and pneumonia as a child and adult. Because I have been blessed with good health, I am curious about the twilight zone between wellness and sickness, the border between life and death. I do not remember ever fearing my own death, as my father had feared his.

I move my head slightly, trying to keep the ice pack on the cut on my scalp. My mind tires of thinking and trails off into reverie . . .

White. Everywhere white. My white skin touching the cold bathroom floor as white as the white swan that Saraswati rides over the heads of musicians playing in a whitewashed room; the flutesong spiraling white into the air like a rope of smoke, joining the chorus of men singing prayers for the beginning of Ramadan; a white crescent moon and a white star pasted on a black sky, and Rani's dark skin across from me while I eat pungent spices of cumin and saffron under the white lights of the Heaven restaurant. Up the stairway to Heaven—does Heaven have stairs? A white lace doily floats down from the sky and turns, twirling so fast it becomes the full moon at the midpoint of Ramadan, midst twenty-nine days of fasting, no food, no drink, only compassion, white as sheets spread out over the earth, while ripples shimmer across the lake waters until very slowly, very softly, out of the blackness appears the white thread of dawn.

Agra
Beauty and the Beloved

Diamonds, pearls, rubies glisten
Like the trickery of a rainbow on the empty horizon,
Soon to vanish like mist
Shedding just
One tear droplet
On the cheek of Time, shining and undefiled—
This Taj Mahal.
—Rabindranath Tagore, "Shah Jahan"

Riding the many hours from Jaipur to Agra in a white Ambassador taxi, I feel pulled by the magnetism of the Taj Mahal. Shankar, our driver, pushes the gas pedal to the floor, impatient to deliver his passengers before nightfall. I am sitting in the back seat of the car, watching the panorama of rural northern India pass by.

I see mustard in bloom, glossing the fields with yellow. Thatched roofs drape over brick houses. Cow-dung patties, laid out in neat rows, dry on the ground, while others, stacked artistically in swirling designs, stand near houses, ready for use as fuel. A woman leans down to lift a heavy sack of grain, briefly holds it horizontally on her bent knees, and then hoists it from her knees to her head and begins walking. Camels clop down the road, pulling rubber-tired carts heaped with goods, mostly logs trailing the back of the carts.

We are traveling on the same highway with the camel carts, lavishly decorated trucks, diesel-smoking buses, cars, scooters, bicyclists, pedestrians, cattle. A ditch filled with stagnant water winds along the highway like a dirty ribbon. A car brakes with a screech to avoid running over sheep—the gold-turbaned shepherd throws up his arms. A generator in a field whines as it pumps water from a well for irrigation. Two boys play, tossing stones in the dirt.

The fields in the countryside are neat, the villages are dirty with bits of debris rolling in the breeze. A skeletal cow rummages through a stack of trash, its tail swatting away flies. Women sit on the ground in front of large mounds of manure and straw, mixing them together to form dung patties. A broken-down Tata truck is stuck smack in the middle of the two-lane highway. No warning. Just stones in the road outlining the truck, its rear axle up on a jack, men trying to repair it. Traffic halts.

A man walks thigh-deep through a pile of millet, his brown legs showing their muscles. Donkeys loaded down with huge sacks of grain plod and nod. Women in colorful saris work, carrying everything on their heads: sticks of wood, pots, branches, stones, clothes, stacks of dung patties and, like the donkeys, sacks of grain. Black cattle stand near their owners' houses in early evening, twitching their ears, a piece of burlap slung over their backs.

We drive past an accident: a collision of bus and jeep. The jeep is completely wrecked. Soldiers push it to the side of the road while the bus juts out into the path of oncoming traffic. Shankar slows the taxi as fog descends over the fields and highway. He says the fog approaching Agra becomes so thick at night that all traffic ceases. Even in the taxi with the windows closed, my nose tingles from the polluted air.

In the town of Agra, lights blaze in a garish glow intensified by the smog. Shankar, still anxious to reach our destination, presses aggressively onward. The streets are filled to capacity with ever-moving, deeply colorful human and animal life. The density of the crowd is so great that the taxi is reduced to inching forward. Faces, turbans, arms, hands, haunches, dark eyes, bodies press against the glass from all sides. A rank odor of air thick with residue from factories seeps into the car. I struggle for breath and feel close to suffocation.

The Taj Mahal is a monument to love. The mausoleum was built by the fifth Moghul emperor, Shah Jahan, a Persian whose name means "king of the world," in memory of his second and favorite wife, Mumtaz Mahal, also a Persian, who died in 1631 giving birth to their fourteenth child. The tenderness of this gesture to capture beauty, love and loss in stone is transferred to all who come to visit the shrine.

Conceived by the minds of the greatest artists of the day as an earthly replica of the Islamic Garden of Paradise, the Taj Mahal, or Crown Palace, is the jewel in an elegant setting of formal gardens. It has become the icon of India, the logo of a land deliciously rich in an enormous variety of traditions. The Taj Mahal is recognized as the culmination of the artistic achievement of the Moghul Empire, many of whose emperors shared an extraordinary sensitivity to and deep love of natural beauty. The Taj Mahal represents a synthesis of architecture from the fourteenth century of Tamerlane to the flowering of seventeenth-century Islamic architecture and design incorporating Hindu and European influences.

Some twenty thousand laborers worked twenty-two years to complete the complex. Architects, designers and craftsmen were brought not only from the entire Muslim world, but also from Europe. Inscriptions from the Qur'an, rendered gloriously in black marble and inlaid in the white arches of the mausoleum and on the tomb itself, were created by the royal calligrapher, the only artist whose signature appears on the monument. Calligraphy is considered the most noble of Islamic arts, for it is the calligrapher who, in transcribing the Qur'an, reproduces the word of God.

The formal gardens with their four channels of water representing the four rivers of Islamic paradise, the accompanying mosque and guesthouse, and the tomb itself create such a harmonious effect that the enormous crowd of tourists from all over the world becomes subdued, entranced by the beauty. It's as if we have all come here to experience something extraordinary, something far beyond our daily existence, and when we arrive, we fall under the spell of this Garden of Paradise.

Shoeless, I join the crowd, as I did at the Lotus Temple in Delhi, and walk the long approach through the formal gardens, following the reflecting pools. My feet are again gliding over marble. Moving with the crowd, I enter the dark tomb itself, which is softly illumined by a single hanging lamp, reminding me of childhood stories of Aladdin. We walk slowly clockwise around a railing, looking down on two elaborately inlaid marble false tombs—a convention in this part of the world—which rest above the vaults where the emperor and empress are buried. I can't ignore the irony that the tomb of Shah Jahan—added after his death and thus not part of the original design—is the one element that throws the impeccable symmetry off balance.

Not until I have walked the long distance to the tomb and returned outside to daylight do I become conscious of the enormous size of the monument. The design of the whole is so graceful that it belies its magnitude. The Moghul emperors had a penchant for the monumental, and on this trip I have seen some of their record-breaking legacies.

Earlier in the day I toured Fatehpur Sikri, the abandoned sixteenth-century Moghul capital built by Emperor Akbar. I saw the huge outdoor courtyard, where Akbar played the ancient game of pachisi, the "board" laid out in rectangular stones large enough to hold the courtesans, who acted as pawns. While Akbar rested on his outdoor throne, he commanded the next move in the game to a courtesan, who glided appropriately over the stones. One thousand concubines lived in Akbar's palace. Huge shopping arcades constructed inside the palace walls allowed the women to buy fabric and jewels to adorn themselves without leaving the palace grounds.

At the Agra Fort I saw the emperor's bathtub, a stone vat big enough to swim in. I was impressed with the largest piece of black onyx in the world, which served as a viewing platform; under its canopy the emperor watched elephant contests and was entertained by the court jester. At the City Palace of Jaipur I had seen two urns, taller than I am, that are the largest sterling silver objects in the world. Not to be outdone by the Moghul emperors, the Maharaja of Jaipur, a devout Hindu, had the giant sterling urns commissioned to carry his personal water supply from the holy Ganges River on his voyage to England.

I admire the grandness of mind of these men of yore, and I wish I knew more about the women. I'm impressed with the insatiable curiosity of the Moghul emperors and the Rajput maharajas, their large appetites for life, their keen appreciation of the natural world. I am touched to read in his *Memoirs* that after a night of love and wine, Babur, the first Moghul emperor, wept at the beauty of a melon, which reminded him of home. I smile at the thought of Jahangir, emperor and father of the man who built the Taj Mahal, bursting into song at the sight of flowers blooming in the meadows of Kashmir. I think of the modest scale and the simplicity with which I have chosen to live my life in contrast to the opulence of Moghul royalty, and rather than feeling diminished, I feel enlarged by the grand scale of these monuments built by men who loved and integrated beauty into their expansive vision.

I linger long in this walled-in earthly paradise. Despite or per-haps because of the crowds, I walk in solitude. I explore the delicate inlays of the colorful floral motifs—semiprecious jewels in white marble. A single leaf requires six green stones of various shading, and the number of leaves is beyond counting. With my fingers I trace an Arabic inscription, black marble in white, Scripture I cannot read but whose elegance of form I can admire. I hold my gaze steady, feasting my eyes on the Crown Palace, captivated by its serene grace and timeless perfection. I wonder when I will return.

In the evening our traveling trio of Rani, Ravi and myself, full to the brim with the sights of Rajasthan and Agra, heads for the railroad station to board the Taj Express and return to Delhi. We go to retrieve our bags from the cloak room, walking past a sign, clearly printed in Hindi and English, "No eatables allowed in luggage because of RATS." Stepping in the near darkness over murky puddles on the cement floor, I find my cloth bag where I put it earlier on the wooden shelf in the farthest room of the luggage den. The required padlock, a miniature version not much bigger than my thumbnail, bought in the station for fifteen rupees, is still attached to the zipper. Reaching to pull my bag off the high shelf, I feel a tug on my sweater and turn to find a small and ragged boy pointing to his stump of an arm. India is a land of contrasts, and within an hour of leaving the imperial wealth of the Taj Mahal I am standing with an impoverished child of today.

When I walk out on the platform to wait for the train I learn that the Taj Express is not running on time. We find a place to stand with our bags and lean up against a large pile of burlap sacks of grain. I watch an old man, sitting on his haunches, drinking his tea and spitting onto the platform. When I look down, out of the corner of my eye I see something moving; slowly in the evening dusk I discern an army of rats, coming and going in busy traffic from the hoard of grain. I grab my bag and step away, trying to focus on the train track, until I am finally rewarded by seeing the Taj Express pull into the station an hour late.

I study the interior of our second-class car—it resembles the design of open European trains with bench seats facing each other. There are metal racks for luggage, and the ceiling is filled with large fans and annoying neon lights. Horizontal bars cover the windows. Other passengers, all Indian, talk for a while and then lean back on the wooden headrests to doze as best they can. We creep our way to Delhi on the Taj Express, the train often stalled on the track for fifteen minutes at a time.

Sitting in the dingy railroad carriage, my mind floats back to my visit to the Taj Mahal. I think of that legacy from the seventeenth century and compare it with what we today are bequeathing our descendents. The town of Agra, home to the Taj Mahal, is now an industrial center filled with coke-based factories that spew enormous amounts of poisonous sulfur dioxide into the air. This settles on the monument as sulfuric acid, flaking the marble and tarnishing its original gleaming white surface. It is the chief pollutant in the air for many miles around.

The Taj Mahal is built along the Yamuna River, now a heavily polluted stream. A thousand yards across the river is another formidable Moghul achievement, the Agra Fort, which contains the Octagonal Tower, where Shah Jahan died. His son, Emperor Aurangzeb, having won the war of succession to the throne of his ailing father by killing his brothers and eliminating the competition, imprisoned his father in the tower for the last seven years of his life. In the seventeenth century, Emperor Shah Jahan had the solace of a clear vista from his prison tower to the monument he built to love, but when I stood, over three centuries later, in the once diamond-encrusted walls of the tower where Shah Jahan had languished, the industrial smog completely obscured the Taj Mahal from view.

Like my Smoky Mountains back home, the region surrounding Agra was once known for its sparkling sky but is now notorious for its heavily polluted air. How far we have strayed in a few centuries from the time of emperors who wept at the sight of a melon and rejoiced at a meadow in bloom!

When the Taj Express finally arrives in Delhi two hours late, at 12:45 A.M., the public phone in the station is locked up for the night. With no way to reach Namgay, who feels now like the patron saint of my visit to India, we force our tired bodies to find a place to spend the night.

We head for the second-class waiting room, and stepping inside the door, we find a carpet of men wrapped in blanket cocoons. We spot three empty orange plastic seats on the opposite side of the room under the windows, and thinking we are in luck, we head for them, stepping as gingerly as we can on the edges of the men's blankets. But the high windows are open, and the stale and bitter night air of Delhi is blowing in. I know I can't last the night in this strong draft, so I open the zipper on my cloth bag, which is stuffed underneath my feet, and pull out the large tablecloth woven of cotton and silk that I bought in Rajasthan. It has a busy elephant design, and I can't help grinning when I unfold the cloth, thinking that these elephants, which I had imagined would grace a dining table back home, are now keeping me warm in a grimy Indian train station. Rani grins, too, and pulls out her tablecloth to cover herself and Ravi.

The neon lights on the ceiling hum an alto drone; the men, asleep on the floor, provide a low, mottled bass with their snoring. The grating voice of a woman on the loudspeaker, announcing in Hindi and English the litany of delayed trains, serves as shrill melody, which blares above our heads throughout the night.

"For the kind attention of the passengers. Train Number *x* from *a* to *b* is now running two hours and thirty minutes late. The inconvenience caused is deeply regretted." The most interesting variations on the theme are the lengths of the delays, which range from two hours to twenty-four hours, and finally, "indefinitely late." I wonder why the stationmaster doesn't simply cross off the day for the train that is twenty-four hours late and cheer up everybody by announcing that the train is on time!

In my lazy, hazy state, crouched in my orange plastic seat, I remember a dream I have had throughout my life: I am running anxiously, rapidly, through countless city streets or over country roads, trying to catch a train that has just pulled out of the station. Each time I have missed that dream train I have awakened, deeply disappointed that I was left behind, that I had missed another opportunity. Watching these snoring men who are waiting for impossibly late trains, I am struck by the irony of it all. The men, like Godot, have spent their days waiting for trains, whereas I have spent my nights dreaming of missing trains, missing opportunities.

This surprises me, for even as a girl, I was eager to try things new. In graduate school I remember Professor Jantz telling his students, "When the goddess Fortuna knocks at your door, seize her by the forelock, for she will disappear as quickly as she appeared. Seize the opportunity when it is there!"

I think of opportunities I have missed, of paths I have not taken. My biggest regret is that I did not fully integrate my early passion for music into my adult life as wife and mother. I remember my piano professor saying to me during my senior year at Oberlin, after I had returned from a year in Munich, that he thought I had lost my focus and discipline to become a performer. I think it was a combination of things: I had discovered other pleasures in the world and was eager to enjoy them, and this gave me an excuse to drop the rigorous, disciplined life of a performer. I think, too, that I fell prey to my doubts that I was not good enough to have a career as a performing artist.

There were other opportunities I didn't pursue in music and travel. The reasons varied, but often it was because I doubted my ability or thought I didn't have adequate preparation. This must have been an innate sense of inadequacy, for my parents were abundantly supportive of all I attempted to do. It must have been the perfectionist in me, holding back. I seem to have had an invisible threshold beyond which I didn't trust myself to go.

In recent years, I have consciously tried to push back old boundaries and keep alert for the unexpected appearance of the goddess Fortuna. I have discovered that even when I've tried something new and failed—like water skiing—I have been enriched by the attempt. The more new things I try, the more invigorated and self-assured I feel.

Rani and I lean up against each other in the Delhi train station to keep warm. As the night smog sails in through the windows behind us, I count the hours until the phone will be unlocked, when I can call Namgay and rejoice in his rescue. Meanwhile, on this night, my last in India, despite the cacophony of the loudspeaker, despite the bad air I am forced to breathe, I renew my resolve to stop missing trains.

"Follow your heart," my old friend Ginny told me when I was newly on my own after my marriage dissolved, "and don't let the excuses in your head get in the way." I followed my heart when I set out on this journey, and today I saw the most beautiful building in the world.

Dhaka
Bangladesh Christmas

> An act of love that fails is just as much a part of
> the divine life as an act of love that succeeds. For
> love is measured by its fullness and not by its
> reception.
>
> —Harold Loucks, British Quaker Educator

Christmas Day in Dhaka, the capital of Bangladesh, feels like summer. Flowers are blooming in the gardens, the air is warm with a slight breeze, and a bright sun brings the day to life. I've just finished hanging out my freshly washed clothes on the roof of Rani's house. The sun will dry them in time for me to change into a fresh dress for Christmas dinner.

Rani and Ravi seem pleased to be back home with William after our travels in India. Rani is indisputably the heart of her home, and she runs her household—wherever she happens to be living—with skill and efficiency. She's a wonderfully intuitive cook, and I like to watch her prepare fresh produce and grains, meat and fish. Today I accompany her to the large market not far from her home to shop for the ingredients for our Christmas dinner.

In the busy food markets of Dhaka the dominant Muslim population is not concerned with Christmas. The trade and bargaining proceed as on any other business day of the week. In the grain market, waist-high sacks of rice, neatly stacked against each other, stand open with their burlap tops rolled back at the edges so that the customers can slide their hands through the kernels to test the moisture and weight of the grains. There are more varieties of rice here than I have ever seen. The merchant talks to Rani in Bangla; they discuss the properties of the different types of rice, and then she chooses a small amount to buy. He weighs the grains on his hanging scale and pours them into her little sack.

I shimmy my way back into the busy crowd. Bright eyes in dark faces stare at me in my black dress, which offsets the rope of local white pearls Rani has given to me as a Christmas present. On the street of the fish market I pass a man frying what looks like a large bass in a huge black iron wok, the fish's eyes staring blindly up at the sky. I stop to buy several small containers of fresh yogurt and tell Rani I want to keep the disposable clay jars, which resemble mini flowerpots. We search out a Chinese merchant so that Rani can buy her special cooking oil. The Chinese woman recognizes Rani, and the two talk together in a halting but effective mixture of languages and gestures. We walk on past the cloth market, where a row of male tailors is busily operating treadle sewing machines on the sidewalk. Further on, I pass stalls of basket weavers selling reed goods that look close in design and material to the baskets made by the Gullah women in Charleston, South Carolina.

When we turn onto the main street, I am suddenly walking against a stream of young girls pouring out of garment factories. Having finished their twelve-hour shift—it is four in the afternoon—operating sewing machines in sweatshops contracted by Western corporations, the girls, who are in their early teens, look happy to be free. In their colorful cottons they chatter with each other as they walk. When I learn they are village girls who have come to the city for employment and live in slums with no electricity or running water, I imagine they will not be hurrying home. Looking up at the factory buildings, I see rows of neon tubes on the ceilings giving off pulsating jabs of vitreous light.

Gathering our parcels together, Rani and I decide to hire a

ricksha to get home. We find a driver waiting next to his bicycle ricksha, and Rani begins to bargain with him. Here in the city where Rani has been living for several years it seems easier for her to bargain than in Rajasthan, where we were traveling as foreign tourists. We climb up onto the seat of the ricksha behind the driver, a man of dignified bearing with gray streaks in his black beard and on his temples. All the rickshas are elaborately painted in designs ranging from jungles and birds to the latest airplanes and movie stars; ours is painted vividly with flowers and has its top pulled back like an open carriage, and for a moment I feel festive, as if we're out for a Sunday drive.

"He won't last two years," Rani says, nodding at the driver. "His diet is too poor to sustain the physical labor of the job. He will get TB." This is followed by the unspoken silence that says, "He will die of it." Rani tells me this as we roll down a dirt path past extensive nurseries along the river. The driver has to pedal standing up to pull us both. The cloth of his tight, white T-shirt is so thin that it is shredding horizontally, exposing slits of brown skin, and the sweat from his exertion glues the worn-out threads to his tired back.

The driver can't understand Rani's English, but I feel uncomfortable because we are talking about the man who is just a few feet in front of us, laboring to pedal us back to a large, comfortable house. When I ask about the lives of ricksha drivers, Rani tells me they are village men who have come to the city as a last resort. The drivers rent the rickshas from the owners, but there are more drivers than rickshas, so a man may be able to work only two or three hours a day. That is not enough to sustain anyone, much less a family. The competition for passengers is severe, not only from other bicycle ricksha drivers, but from the drivers of motorized rickshas and cars, who would like to see the bicycle rickshas banned so that they can have all the business to themselves.

Even though our ricksha moves smoothly and quietly down the tree-lined road, its technical design is old-fashioned and inefficient, and I remark on this to Rani. She tells me that a major effort was made to introduce a well-designed ricksha with bicycle gears, altered seat position and improved balance, but the owners rejected it. My logic tells me there must be a solution that could benefit all sides and the environment, too. A well-designed bicycle ricksha could give fuller employment to many men, reduce their likelihood of succumbing to tuberculosis, use no noxious fuel and cause no air pollution or noise.

I think how difficult it can be to effect positive change, but if there's a will, there's a way. The twentieth century has given us models of people who persisted against seemingly insurmountable odds and triumphed in their cause: Mahatma Gandhi, Martin Luther King and Nelson Mandela, to name only three. And women like Mary Robinson, former President of Ireland and now United Nations High Commissioner for Human Rights, have shown that women are capable of inspired leadership. I think, too, of the Peace Pilgrim, the nameless woman who spent decades of her life walking thousands of miles to spread her message of peace.

When we reach the high gate to Rani's house, she pays the driver and suggests she take a picture of me and the driver in front of the ricksha. The driver quickly agrees; within seconds a beggar and a boy appear from nowhere, grinning and wanting to be in the photo. I was the self-conscious one in that picture because I was not comfortable with the great disparity of means between the threadbare ricksha driver and beggar and myself, sporting my lovely new Christmas pearls.

Inside the house Rani takes charge of her kitchen domain, preparing Christmas dinner. She asks me to make the crust for the pie filling she has cooked from a fresh local pumpkin and gives me a handmade wooden rolling pin, much thinner and smaller than the one I use at home. While I work with the pie dough, Rani mashes the pumpkin with a wooden masher that looks like an eight-pointed star on the end of a long wooden handle.

Finally, Christmas dinner is served, and the four of us gather around the dining table to enjoy roast chicken with new potatoes, steamed cauliflower, cucumber slices and fresh pumpkin pie topped with ice cream, all ingredients bought at stalls in the local market. Everything is delicious. I feel relaxed and pleased to be celebrating Christmas with my good friends.

When the phone rings, I am surprised to see William hand me the receiver. It is my aunt Mary, calling from Washington, D.C. During the twenty-six years since my mother's death, I have developed a closeness to my aunt, as if she has taken over where my mother left off. She is thirty years older than I am, just as I am thirty years older than my daughter. Sometimes I imagine the three of us, marching in step through the years, like drum majorettes leading a band, each thirty years apart. Ninety, sixty, thirty. Old age, middle age, youth. I see myself reflected in both my aunt and my daughter, giving me the luxury of visually imagining my old age as well as remembering my youth.

My aunt has the calm staying power of a redwood tree—tall, erect, lovely in her old age. Her faith in the goodness of human beings does not waver as she tirelessly makes sandwiches for the homeless and brings solace to friends in need. Her clarity of insight into the causes of conflict makes her a source of counseling for all in the family. Now over the phone she wishes me a good Christmas, and I hear a tremor in her voice as it trails off and the connection is broken.

I imagine my daughter back in New York. She continues with her firm grip on life, just as after her birth, her tiny hand instinctively made a fist around her father's outstretched finger. Ellen was my rebel child, her strong sense of self emerging from the minute she was able to sit up in a high chair and spit her first volley of strained spinach in my face. I remember her second grade teacher telling me that Ellen was unique. When the teacher asked the pupils in her class to write down the name of the child they would most like to play with, more children chose Ellen than anyone else, and Ellen wrote "myself"—the only pupil, her teacher assured me, who had ever given that response.

The phone call from my aunt has stirred up memories, but when Rani offers me a second piece of pumpkin pie, I have no trouble returning to the present.

The Dhaka I see today is a modern version of a settlement that began a thousand years ago. Its glory days were in the seventeenth century, when it served as the capital of Bengal, the easternmost extension of the Moghul Empire. Previously recognized with the Romanized spelling of Dacca, the city has been capital of the Indian state of Bengal, as well as of East Pakistan. Today it is capital of the People's Republic of Bangladesh, which won its independence from Pakistan in a brutal civil war in 1971.

Bangladesh, slightly smaller than the state of Wisconsin, is one of the poorest nations of the world, with the staggering population of some 130 million. In 1971, Bangladesh received media attention in the West when rock stars and musicians from many countries staged the Concert for Bangladesh in Madison Square Garden, raising millions of dollars for UNICEF's relief efforts to aid the starving and those made homeless by the country's civil war. Even on my short visit to the capital, I detect an ardent spirit of freedom, which we hear little of in the Western press. National monuments pay generous homage to the martyrs who gave their lives to wrest the country from the control of Great Britain and then Pakistan.

Rani and her family live in the modern section of Dhaka called Ramna. Instead of going into the old city to view the remnants of the Moghul Empire or some of the hundreds of Islamic mosques, Ravi and I hop in the car with Rani's husband, William, behind the wheel. We head first for the American Embassy, where Rani works as a nurse. The embassy looks like a modern fort made of brick and surrounded by tall walls. Loaded oil drums, defining a tightly meandering path to the parking lot, serve as a barrier to prevent cars from speeding up to the entrance. This is no elegant diplomatic outpost, but an armed fortification in foreign territory built to withstand acts of terrorism against the United States.

William drives to the center of Dhaka to the National Parliament Building. Commissioned in 1962 by the Pakistan government when Bangladesh was the eastern wing of a divided Pakistan, the modern "megaproject" was designed by the American architect Louis Kahn. The building is a huge structure of concrete, marble and brick, but even from a distance I notice something unusual: large geometric cutouts—triangles, circles, squares—that look as if they were excised from the concrete walls by giant cookie cutters. Located on a branch of the Dhaleswari River, the massive structure floats above the water on three sides. Large, round, red-brick towers, also on the water, serve as apartment buildings for government workers. The spaciousness of the enormous complex is reminiscent of the large scale the Moghul emperors employed centuries before. It is a feat of modern politics that the Parliament Building was finally dedicated in 1983, twelve years after the new nation of Bangladesh had won its independence from Pakistan.

On this warm, sunny day William and I walk at a leisurely pace through a large public garden, while Ravi runs ahead. William is a public servant of the highest caliber, not in politics, but in medicine. Whether he is setting up a new medical clinic in a rural mountain county of North Carolina, heading a program in Nigeria to improve the health of children suffering from diarrheal diseases, or working with the World Health Organization here in Bangladesh, he thinks on a public scale.

Over the years William has encouraged me to pick up the thread of service in my own life that began in my early days of Quaker work camps in Philadelphia and Germany. He is fond of suggesting that I apply for a post teaching music in a private school in India or teaching English at a university in China. Each time this conversation comes up, I am tempted; my belief in humanitarian service, my love of travel and living in a new culture spring to the fore. Like William and Rani, I could become involved in international service work abroad and lead a rich and varied life in many countries. But upon reflection, I find at this stage of life I am more interested in playing out my creative talent in music and writing, perhaps to compensate for the musical career I never had.

In the evening William, Rani and Ravi take me as their guest to a party of U.N. people held at a Chinese couple's home. The house is buzzing with activity—children are playing, guests are talking and singing. Standing by a table of holiday food lit with candles, I talk with a silver-haired Indian man and a stocky Slavic woman. Both have compassionate hearts, and in answer to my questions, they tell me about their work. The Indian man says that, as we speak, people in the former Soviet republics are tearing their furniture and houses apart, bit by bit, to burn for heat. The people have no fuel or running water, and winter has arrived. He looks directly at me when he says he knows that many of those people will not live through the winter.

The Slavic woman, whose husband and children live in Australia, has recently worked with refugees in Bosnia. One of her tasks was to supply the people with large plastic sheeting to use as a barrier against the cold in lieu of walls and roofs destroyed in the war. In one place, a baby had just been born, and the infant's mother used the sheeting to protect her newborn daughter from the December cold. The plastic sheeting served as her baby's swaddling clothes.

Both the Indian man and the Slavic woman, like William, know that what they are doing is far from enough. They know their aid is inadequate for the countless people who need help, yet they don't give up. I think of how often on this trip I have felt overwhelmed by the suffering of the world's people and of the planet itself, but I must not forget the people of good will everywhere, like those in this room, who are devoting their lives to making a better world.

I move to the edge of the room and stand listening to the Christmas carols the host is playing on the piano. The wine and good company warm my heart. I look about the room and see people of numerous nationalities, races, creeds, talking together with a common purpose, all working to alleviate human misery in some of the most desolate regions of the earth. Their compassion is infectious, and for a moment in this Chinese home in Dhaka, Bangladesh, the light of the flickering candles and the harmony of the Christmas music fill me with hope.

Singapore
Confronting the Challenge

In the service of life sacrifice becomes grace.
—Albert Einstein, *The World As I See It*

I am breathing moist tropical air, and I taste no pollution. It is pouring rain, the first I've seen since Zurich, only here the rain is warm and gentle, without wind. This is the closest I have ever been to the equator, just one degree north. I'm in Singapore and it's five-thirty in the morning.

I was able to check through three of my four bags to Hawaii, so I can travel light here on the island. It is still dark as I make my way through the ultramodern air terminal and find the bus connection to my hotel. Already I am impressed with the courtesy and efficiency of the employees and the cleanliness of the airport—a remarkable contrast to my experiences in Delhi. This small island nation spent much of the twentieth century climbing out of poverty, and thanks to the determined efforts of former prime minister Lee Kuan Yew, an autocratic, no-nonsense leader, Singapore has forced its way into economic prosperity.

Settled in my modern, high-rise hotel, I pause within the quiet, soft coral walls of the room to get my bearings. I have been with people for a long stretch, and now I need to readjust, not only to a new place, but to being alone again. I welcome the solitude and the time to assimilate the many sights and sensations I have experienced along the way.

Midmorning, I step out into the tropical rain to explore my new surroundings. I take a long walk up one side of Orchard Road and down the other. Over the years I have heard a lot about Singapore from Asian international students I've hosted in the States, who stop here on their way home to load up on electronic gadgets and Western manufactured goods at cheap prices. Orchard Road is a long line of department stores and specialty shops—the same stores one finds in any urban shopping mall in the United States. Well-dressed men and women cruise down the broad cement sidewalks, carrying full shopping bags bearing the logos of Parisian and New York City stores. European and American children toting expensive toys run after their overweight parents. I catch myself staring at the heavyset people, who stand out after the trim and thin populations I have been among. They, like the overstocked stores, seem excessive.

In this cosmopolitan city, restaurants of many nations, open and waiting for business, are interspersed among the stores. For no particular reason I walk down a small flight of steps into an Italian bistro and find a table against the wall, sitting below ground. I look up at the small windows and see rain splashing into the window wells. The space is a bit of Italy, re-created in warm wood with scenes of Tuscany on the wall. I order a bowl of minestrone and a glass of Chianti. The Italian waiter brings a long, thin loaf of crusty, white bread, wrapped in a red napkin and presented in a wine glass. I listen to arias from *Rigoletto* being piped into the dark room while I spread sweet butter on the warm bread. The rich, hot soup full of vegetables and pasta satisfies my hunger, yet something is missing.

Walking outside within the carefully delineated crosswalk and obeying the clear pedestrian signals, I move to the other side of Orchard Road toward the Singapore National Library. Inside is a hive of well-dressed students and adults studying and working at computers. No quaint library of poorly lit reading rooms as I found in Nepal, no card catalog, but rather a modern online catalog and databases, very close to what is in my university library back home. Many books in English line the shelves of the bright, orderly and spotless library.

I continue my walk in the rain. Signs in English reminding people of good conduct are everywhere. "Vandalism is a crime. Offenders will be apprehended by the police" is posted in the window of a McDonald's. In the Singapore government's attempt to pull the island population out of the poverty and accompanying squalor commonplace in Asia, it has passed laws against behaviors deemed offensive to the march of progress. Chewing gum is prohibited because people use gum to jam locks and because wads of discarded chewing gum dirty the sidewalks and streets. Littering and spitting are taboo. Signs I saw posted at regular intervals in the neatly cut grass along the clean highway entering town remind drivers not to cut back and forth between lanes. I feel as if I have landed in a real-life Disney World and am torn between admiring the orderliness and wishing for a sign of authenticity.

Hoping for a taste of the tropical island this is, I take a bus tour out to the Jurong Bird Park, where I amble in the rainy afternoon past caged birds from all over the world. Penguins swim in tanks of cold water; large golden carp preen among water lilies. I listen to the tour guide try to convey to his phlegmatic charges his enthusiasm for the birds, their gorgeous plumage, their native habitats in varying climates and altitudes, their ways of mating and finding food. But what interests the tourists is buying plastic reproductions of flamingos and rubber snakes in the park's gift shop.

Walking alone in the rain past the tallest flight cages, I look for the large birds of prey hiding in the foliage. I wonder if they are as depressed about being caged in a foreign land as I am distressed about being in this small, seemingly artificial, island nation. It's not the rain getting me down and it's not the hearty Italian meal. It must be the busloads of prosperous tourists who scurry to buy luxury goods at discount prices in this land of plenty. Singapore is a shopper's paradise, but I am not a shopper of mass-produced goods.

For the last forty days I have been steeped in rural cultures that are still, to a great extent, representative of indigenous tradition. The old ways predominate, local languages and dialects flourish, the majority of people communicate orally rather than through writing. Buildings are constructed from the natural materials at hand, and the food eaten is what the people have grown and harvested themselves. Goods are transported on the backs of the people and their beasts of burden. When the local cultures are not largely intact, it is often due to Western industries that have moved in to take advantage of cheap labor——factories that take from the cities and towns, but give little that is beneficial in return.

I am not romanticizing the poverty I've seen throughout Asia. Rather, I am confronting the reality of my own American culture, which I see mirrored here in this miniature nation. In Singapore I am witnessing an example of the homogenization of the world's cultures by the creeping consumerism of capitalism. I realize with dismay that the same economic prosperity I see around me is the basis of the American Dream. This copycat nation, the "success story" of Asia, has broken free of poverty, ensuring its citizens a decent living. While this is an admirable achievement, the excessive consumption, as in the United States, is a hollow victory.

The original intent of my globe-circling celebration was to experience for myself the beauty and the fullness of the planet where I live. But here in Singapore, the deeper implications of my travel impressions are bubbling to the surface, and I feel uneasy.

We, the rich people of the world, desperately need a change in direction, a change of heart. We need to sacrifice our superfluous luxuries that are robbing the earth and depriving the poor. We need to listen to the ancient wisdom of tribal societies, whose reverence for the natural world nourished the earth rather than destroyed it. Those of us who yearn for profound harmony with the earth and its peoples must speak out and take action in our daily lives. We must show our children and grandchildren that by living in peace with one another and by employing earth-friendly technologies we can enjoy a simplified and healthy lifestyle compatible with the world around us.

In the early evening I walk again along the streets, now illuminated by white lights that have been strung in the trees and over bushes to add a festive touch for the Christmas holidays. I am caught off guard by my reaction to Singapore and want to turn my thinking in a positive direction. As I consider the immense task before us of reversing human exploitation of the planet, I think that we women are peculiarly suited to the challenge. If we remember that many early societies were matriarchal, composed of peoples who revered the earth as a nourishing mother and who accorded women full respect for their wisdom as well as their bodies, that can give us courage.

Brave women in many countries have reversed their destinies by asserting their rights. They have restored to women the freedom and power to fully develop their potential. I think of one woman, Rachel Carson, my fellow alumna from Johns Hopkins, who observed and described the beauty of sea life and warned the world in the 1960s about the destructive consequences of using commercial insecticides. While my contribution to making a better world will certainly not be the same as hers, Rachel Carson's work inspires me and reminds me that each of us can make a difference.

Walking in the rain of Singapore, I drink in the moisture. I'm south of the Tropic of Cancer and can taste it on my lips.

• • •

The hum of the plane traveling north fills my head. It surrounds me with its vibrations, cradles me in its rough, deep monotone and helps to keep me in the low gear I prefer to be in on long flights.

Crimped in my narrow window seat, I take stock of my body and the marks it bears from my journey. Two purple toenails from the trek down Pulchowki mountain. Left shin scab, compliments of a desert jeep's bumper. Bruise on my belly from colliding with a marble chest in the City Palace of Jaipur. Scabs on my scalp from the night I fainted in Udaipur. Old bump on my head from hitting the low gate in Kathmandu. Dark bruise behind my left knee, courtesy of a baby stroller in the Delhi airport. A cough that keeps trying to rid my lungs of the polluted air of Asian cities.

Markings from the road. I close my eyes and concentrate on the engine's roar.

Deplaning in Seoul, Korea, I am greeted at the end of the catwalk by a beautiful flight attendant dressed in the bright-red uniform of Korean Air. She has been charged with finding me and leading me to my connecting flight. It had not occurred to me that I would not find my own way.

"You travel alone?" she asks sympathetically in her clear school English. "Yes," I reply, watching her look over my tickets. She leads me away from the crowd to a counter where she can inspect my papers. "Follow me," she says, and we begin to walk down long corridors together.

"Where is your family?" she asks, when we have walked several yards. "Back home in the United States," I say, thinking that is enough to satisfy her curiosity. "Where is your husband?" she tries again, hoping to find out more. "I am not married," I say.

"But you are on a long, long trip by yourself?" she asks. When I confirm this, I can see the sympathy in her eyes when she says, "I am so sorry. I am so sorry you travel alone."

I try to tell the attendant she need not be sorry, I like being on my own and there are always people around me I can talk to, if I wish. But her face has lost its smile and looks pensive. She leads me to an old freight elevator in which we descend slowly to ground level. Soon we are walking out on the tarmac, where the noise from the engines drowns out any attempt at conversation. She leads me to a large, empty bus, and we climb in its open doors. She speaks a few words in Korean to the driver, who turns with a sad look in my direction. He closes the bus doors, and we are off, driving across the tarmac past planes painted with diverse colorful logos.

"I am sad for you," the stewardess in red says as she watches me from across the bus aisle. "I am sad you do not have friend or family to travel with." By now her expression is genuinely downcast, and I wonder if it is worth my effort to try to explain further. I smile as best I can to show her I am having a good time. When we reach the area where my next plane departs, she helps me off the bus, as if I am an old lady. I begin to wonder if I have aged terribly in the last few days. I thank her warmly, and she departs with the saddest look in her eyes.

Sitting in the huge hall waiting for my flight to Honolulu, I think about the young woman in red. It seems her idea of being alone is equivalent to being an outcast, someone without family or friends. One of the big differences between the cultures of Asia and Africa and the cultures of the West is that the Westerner, particularly the American, thinks in terms of the individual—individual freedom, individual rights, individual privacy—while the Asian and African see themselves as an integral part of their family, their society. They are absorbed in communal living: arranged marriages, the extended family where many generations live together, the young obeying the wishes of the old. In Asia and Africa the actions of an individual reflect—for better or for worse—upon the group, bringing fame or shame to the family or society. In America, respect for individual freedom has diminished the importance of the group, even such a fundamental social unit as the family. Perhaps the Korean stewardess misunderstood my independence for loneliness and isolation, because she could not imagine a woman in her society traveling without family or friend.

I watch the steady stream of Koreans walking by my chair and notice that no one looks at me. No one comes close to looking me in the eye—not even the small children—and I find this remarkable. They walk past me as if I am a statue—quite the opposite from the Bangladeshis, who stared openly at me—yet the Koreans communicate in lively fashion among themselves.

To my left sits an older woman, chewing and spitting on the floor. One particularly large volley lands an inch from my shoe. I look up at her, but she stares straight ahead, as if I weren't here. I try to imagine what's going on in her mind, for I know she feels my presence, just as I feel hers. I wonder if that salvo of sputum was meant for my shoe.

Throngs of Korean tourists returning from their holiday stream past me with bags stuffed with goods—as full as any I saw on Orchard Road in Singapore. My own bags are filled with presents I have bought on this trip—handmade crafts from the countries I have visited, but goods nonetheless. Gradually the Koreans around me pick up their bags and leave, one by one, so that I am left by myself on the bench, looking out into the dark. The tall windows against the night sky serve as mirrors, and I see myself, sitting alone in the large hall.

These are my last moments in Asia, a continent so vibrant with life, so rich in paradox. I wish I could convince the stewardess in red that I loved my stay here, that I wouldn't have missed my solo journey for the world.

Hawaii
A Lei a Day

> In a place of beauty there is also great power.
> —Thomas Rain Crowe, "Poem from Paradise"

If paradise means being happy in a beautiful place, then I am in paradise. Standing on the shore of the Kona Coast on the Big Island of Hawaii, I feel as if I have arrived in the mythical State of Delight. The sun sparkles on the azure blue of the Pacific, and powerful breakers crash on the black lava rocks, sending extravagant white plumes of spray into the clear blue air. The wind blows my hair clean of all the pollutants it has suffered for the past six weeks. I stand firmly on a volcanic island anchored to the floor of the sea, thousands of miles from any continent, thousands of miles from cities jammed with people.

The gray haze of disillusion that hovered over me in Singapore is swept from my mind. My tiredness from being en route for twenty-four hours is slipping away, like a dark cloak falling from my shoulders. I can't stop smiling. The young college student who drove me to my hotel was laid back and friendly. The staff of the Royal Kona Resort does everything to make me feel at home. Fountains splash in the courtyard. Parrots preen in the sunlit vegetation of the garden. All I hear is the sound of water and wind.

I find a small, attractive clothes shop and buy a blue Indonesian batik dress with easy slits at the sides and a pair of rubber Pali Hawaiian sandals. I sip a glass of mango juice on a sunny terrace. I watch the native Hawaiians move with an easy grace, their limbs flowing as in a dance. No rush. And why should they hurry? They are here, now, in this beautiful place, and have no need to think about going elsewhere. They have arrived!

I'm thankful to be spending this first day here in Hawaii by myself. I want the quiet time, the chance to absorb the beauty without distraction. I sit on a rock and watch the ocean tide fill the lagoon and the multicolored fish enjoy the shallow water. I watch the foam disperse after each wave crashes on the lava rocks and then gradually ebbs out to sea. My eyes come to rest on the clear horizon, blue on blue, where sky meets sea. In my fantasy, it is the rim of the world, holding me gently on this peaceful isle.

I watch a boy and girl play on the sand, totally absorbed in building their castle, and I wish I had spent more of my life building castles in the sand. It is an art to be content in paradise. Children know how. Animals know. And some older people remember how. But very few adults in midlife know. We get distracted, thrown off course, embroiled in the heat of our emotions. We don't even see the trees around us. One thing leads to another, and before we know it, our life is almost over.

The most important thing I had wanted to share with my children was the joy of life, and I think I succeeded. The hallmark of Ellen's personality is her joy, her love of spontaneity. After Peter died, what I heard again and again was that Peter's legacy to his friends was his joy of life. What my children prize most—joy, the moment, friends—I also prize. Peter had told one of his friends, shortly before he died, that he thought the best stage of life was childhood. I'm glad Peter understood. I'm grateful Peter and Ellen shared those innocent years of childhood with each other.

A sense of longing envelops me, wraps around me like the cloth of my sky-blue batik. I long for that time of innocence when I was content as a child—content to explore the world around me, content to play. A good childhood is a state of grace. It can't be far from the enlightenment that is the goal of spiritual seekers. And it must be akin to the lifestyle of peoples of warm climes, like the natives here in Hawaii, who have all they need of beauty and food and shelter to sustain them.

The island peoples of Tahiti taught Paul Gauguin, the world-weary French painter, how to live, how to be present in the moment. It is such an easy thing to do, if we can only let go of the restraints tying us down. Think of Gulliver in his travels, pinned to the ground with hundreds of threads by the Lilliputians, who held him captive. In truth, we hold ourselves captive, pinned down by the threads of our desires.

I'm holding on tight to Thomas, sitting on the back of a moped, heading for the southernmost tip of the United States. This seems a dubious claim, for the Hawaiian islands are sufficient unto themselves. It feels inappropriate to say that these elegant mid-Pacific islands belong to the military-industrial power of the United States. Thomas and I are headed for South Point, the southernmost tip of Hawaii.

Our moped sails along Highway 11, past coffee plantations, past beaches, moving south to open road. We gradually bear to the east, then turn right onto South Point Road, which becomes narrow and winding, full of swells in the cracked, old pavement. We pass a few simple country homes and a field of windmills harnessed to a power station. The road becomes stony and finally disappears into a rocky beach.

We park the moped on the pebbly soil and begin exploring the ruins of an ancient settlement—canoe moorings, a ceremonial ground with flower offerings, indicating that it is still in use, a plat-form for raising nets of fish up the cliff from the sea. We find a warm place on the porous lava rocks to sit and eat our cheese and fruit.

We are still looking at each other shyly, getting reacquainted after seven weeks apart. Thomas looks at my short hair, which he has not seen on me before, and I smile to see him in a new Hawaiian shirt and shorts, both in patterns I could not imagine him wearing. I feel as if I am on the honeymoon with him that we never had. Coming together as older adults, having met after we each had already lived full lives, we dispensed with the ritual of marriage and took up housekeeping together because we had found kindred spirits in each other and wanted to share the many creative pursuits we had in common.

When Thomas arrived in Hawaii, his first words to me were, "Who are you?" He is always direct and gets straight to the point. I couldn't answer his question then, but just smiled and gave him a big hug.

"I am both the same and changed," I thought, resting my legs on a warm rock. My character has not changed, but this circular journey has given me a larger perspective, enriched me and raised my tolerance a notch. I have been allowed to share in the domestic life of people who live vastly different lives from my own, and I cel-ebrate those differences. I have seen glimpses of the globe at the end of the twentieth century that reveal a Paradise Lost, and I want to do what I can to help regain that paradise.

When Thomas points to the sky in the west, I see large black clouds coming our way. We pack up the remains of our lunch and return to our moped to begin the long drive back to the hotel, but the storm is traveling faster than we can move, and soon we are overtaken by wind and rain. We pause at a picnic ground, briefly taking shelter, but seeing the storm grow in size, we decide to head back out to the road. Without any protection from the weather, we press on, the cold drops of rain stinging our faces, arms and legs. The trip back feels much longer than the trip down as the wind pastes our cold, wet clothes to our skins. This is island weather—sudden changes in climate. A few miles to the east are the volcanoes we saw the day before, heaving hot steam and vivid red molten lava from the ground, and here we are freezing on a moped in the rain!

Even without my glasses I can spot the sign to the coffee planta-tion. As if he were reading my mind, Thomas pulls off the road and up to the entrance. We take shelter inside the plantation store and are greeted by the aroma of freshly roasted coffee—Kona coffee—some of the best beans anywhere. A woman offers us mugs to serve ourselves from a large pot on the counter. We stand in the warmth of the store sipping the brew, a robust flavor with high caffeine con-tent. I feel the kick of the drug giving a jump-start to my heart, and my mood picks up. Surely, I say, this storm will pass.

Within half an hour we are on our way back to the hotel. After a warm shower and change of clothes, Thomas and I walk down the road to a little cart where a local woman sells leis. She beams when she sees Thomas coming—he has been one of her best cus-tomers this week. On the first day of our reunion he presented me with a lei of pink orchids and announced he would give me a lei a day as long as we stayed on this island paradise. A poet and gardener with a high appreciation for beauty, Thomas takes his time discussing with the woman which lei will be the choice for today, which will look best on the dress I am wearing. She appraises me with a shrewd eye, and hands him a specially woven rope of dark green leaves plaited in an intricate design, highlighted by a few soft pink plumeria blossoms. The woman's son, sitting nearby, says with a gentle Hawaiian lilt in his voice, that he has tried many times to plait a similar lei, but the design is too intricate.

Thomas drapes the laced leaves and flowers around my shoulders, making sure they fall onto my back and can be seen well from behind. What can I give in return but a smile that wells from deep within my heart.

The natives call it "Pu'uhonua o Honaunau": Place of Refuge of Honaunau, sacred ground on which life could begin anew. Anyone who had broken a sacred law (*kapu*) could escape certain death by finding refuge here and receiving absolution from the priest (*kahuna pule*) before returning home. In the sixteenth century the temple housing the sacred bones of dead chiefs lent sanctity to the area. The early Hawaiians believed a special power (*mana*) resided with the royal line of high chiefs. The palace grounds of the chief are separated from the place of refuge by a massive stone wall some thousand feet long and ten feet high. The great wall not only separated but joined the people within the sanctuary by giving them hope for a second chance at life.

Situated on the west coast of the island of Hawaii, this refuge, the last of its kind, comprises 180 acres along a Pacific shore lined with palm trees and a reconstruction of some of the buildings on the original sacred site. I've come here to honor the native peoples, past and present, and to take time for my own thoughts as I prepare to leave this last stop on my voyage.

The native peoples of these islands prospered here long before they were found by outsiders. They constructed a religion that was appropriate for their own land, their own set of circumstances. They believed the natural catastrophes of tidal waves, lava flows and earthquakes were brought down upon their people by gods angry that their sacred laws had been broken by acts of irreverence to the chief or by the inability of the weak to fight in battle.

In every land I have visited on this journey, I have discovered that the people find the ways and means of being devout that suit their circumstances. I have seen Hindus honor the cow, because in ancient times the cow fed their people life-giving milk. I have seen Buddhists honor the poor, because the Buddha taught them compassion for the sufferings of their fellow human beings. I have seen a Catholic church stripped of its ornamentation by Protestants, who protested the excesses of the Roman church. I have seen Muslims protect their women, following the command of their prophet Muhammad. Everywhere I go I see people worshiping in a way that they feel speaks to their condition and that often retains practices that seem outmoded today. My own Quaker way of life once practiced simplicity of speech and clothing in response to the rigid class structure and hoarded wealth maintained by the Church of England.

Despite the outward signs of the various religions, I believe there is a core that transcends the ephemera of customs. Behind the worship of the cow is a Hindu reverence for a life-sustaining animal. Behind the simplicity of a church or meetinghouse is the ideal that people don't need expensive structures in order to worship. In Emily Dickinson's words:

> Some keep the Sabbath going to Church –
> I keep it, staying at Home –
> With a Bobolink for a Chorister –
> And an Orchard, for a Dome –

Seeing the multitude of organized religions the peoples of the world have developed over thousands of years does not lessen my own belief. It only reminds me that to move forward with others, I must transcend the surface differences that divide us.

I feel the sacredness of the Place of Refuge, not because I am a descendent of the native peoples who believed in gods who punished errant ways with earthquakes and fiery volcanoes, but because it is a place of natural beauty, a part of the creation into which I was born. Like Emily Dickinson, I don't feel the need of a temple, a stupa, a mosque, a cathedral or a meetinghouse to worship. I can offer a prayer just as easily here on this lava beach as the camel driver did on the sand dune in the Thar Desert.

Along the stony beach I watch the turtles with their sophisticated camouflage move among the rocks and seaweed. How brilliant the designs on their backs! How incomparable the artistry of animal, plant, mineral! With so much beauty, with so many diverse and wondrous species on our earth, how can we possibly doubt the truth of a grand design that includes us all?

Under the early evening sky as the full moon emerges above the crashing surf and then bids languid farewell to the horizon, I remember the moon in the Chagall painting I saw in Zurich. Two moons have waxed and waned while I've been on my round-the-world journey. One rose over the Himalaya, as I emerged on the elephant from the jungle in Nepal, and the other is rising now above the expanse of the deep blue Pacific, leaving a trail of light on the water rolling toward shore.

Standing at the water's edge, where the sea makes love to the shore, I feel the wind tousle my hair and billow my full skirt about me. I breathe in the fresh air that has swept across the sea to this island of volcanic rock. My joy brims to overflowing.

Tuckasegee
Full Circle

> No journey carries one far unless, as it extends
> into the world around us, it goes an equal distance
> into the world within.
>
> —Lillian Smith, *The Journey*

Back home in the mountains of western North Carolina, winter has settled over the land. The trees on Shelton Mountain are bare, their dark branches moving slowly in the January wind. The gardens are at rest; only the heather stands out, wearing red, deep green and creamy yellow in its various shades of winter dress. Cardinals, snowbirds and titmice visit the feeders.

My journey has come full circle, and thus to its end, yet my body, sensing the halting of the motion of travel, still yearns for the openness to new adventure I have had these last two months on the road. "My favorite thing is to go where I've never been." I feel the way the photographer Diane Arbus must have felt when she wrote that—a physical longing to keep moving, each day discovering new things.

As if to assuage my restless spirit, I don my yak-wool coat and walk up into the winter field above my house, past the blackberry brambles, past the sleeping dogwood and black walnut trees, past the bits of locust shooting up everywhere. I walk on the mowed path through tall, dry grasses up to the top of the field and then turn and look out over the stark winter valley. Below, the Tuckasegee

River, whose Cherokee name means "tortoise," flows evenly along the roadside at the foot of the hill. The old farmhouse where I live sits nestled in a small grove of tall trees. The only movement is the river, making its way from its spring in the mountains above, past fields and houses like mine, past towns and cities to the sea.

The sun, concealed most of the morning, breaks through the clouds and brings warmth to the field. Wanting to stay outdoors, I walk back down the mowed path, across the dry creek bed to my favorite rock, a flat chunk of granite large enough for me to stretch out and sleep on. Today I am content to sit on the rock, to feel its solid surface beneath me. I want to watch and listen and become reacquainted with my hospitable patch of earth.

I look down toward the old farmhouse with the tin roof and know that I can be happy here with Thomas, sharing the daily rituals of chores, enjoying meals together. I look forward to the spontaneity we have working together on literary and musical projects. I look forward to the weekend afternoons when we set out in his truck, picnic basket in hand, to find another new spot by a waterfall or a knoll with a view, where we spread out our blanket and take time to enjoy our tea.

I will return to my reference work in the library, where I have been helping students with their questions for sixteen years, trying to teach them to think critically about the answers. I will drive the same stretch of winding road along the Tuckasegee River each morning, but instead of following the road to discover new places, I'll return home to this rock, these fields, this old farmhouse and garden, where my discoveries each day will be in my own back yard. I'll read and walk and talk with friends. I'll get lost in my music, discovering new places, new vistas in my mind. Then, when the season is right, I will don my traveling shoes again.

• • •

The rock I am sitting on is hard, but if I arrange the yak wool of my coat beneath me, it keeps me warm and comfortable. On a clear day like this, it's best to be outdoors on the mountain. The freshness of the winter air clears the cobwebs from my mind and makes it easy for me to think. This is dream time, memory time.

Last June, before embarking on my solo trip around the world, I took a sentimental journey north and west. I drove alone, three thousand miles, in a loop that took me as far north as Michigan and as far west as the Mississippi. Taking the trip alone was an act of faith as well as a test of myself to see if I could do it. I wanted to see how self-sufficient I could be.

I drove first to Washington, D.C., to spend leisurely days with my cousin and aunt, contemplating with pleasure the familiar gestures and lilt of voices I had known since childhood. I spent a day talking, eating, cruising on a pontoon boat around a lake in a rendezvous with my daughter, whose radiant smile fueled my mother's heart. With renewed energy, I drove out to Oberlin, Ohio, where I walked the flat, summer-quiet streets of my old college town and found a Steinway grand in a conservatory practice room. I was surprised when I heard my fingers spontaneously playing, "I Am a Poor Wayfaring Stranger." The liquid sounds coming from the old piano seemed to embrace all the years of my girlhood and womanhood in one lyrical moment.

I continued to the upper peninsula of Michigan, where I stayed in my sister Marnie's old cottage on a bay, having the luxury of private quarters during a family reunion. We sisters and cousins played together, even frolicked like the kids we once were, boating, walking, talking, as if there were no tomorrow. Those few days together renewed the solidarity of spirit I have always felt with my family.

Continuing westward, I pursued the shorelines of Lake Huron and then Lake Michigan to return to Door County, Wisconsin, where I had summered with my husband and children for thirty years. Returning alone for the first time since the breakup of my family, I drove past my husband's tree-lined driveway, saw his white car parked by the day lilies I used to admire, but I didn't stop, knowing he would not stop for me. I walked for an hour along the beach, where I used to run with my children, and took a freezing dip alone in the waters of Lake Michigan. I recovered from the cold with a warm supper of chowder and lake perch at Al Johnson's Swedish Restaurant, where my husband and I used to celebrate our anniversaries. I spent the evening sitting on a wooden porch, watching the late-night sunset dissolve over the waters of Green Bay before falling into a deep sleep.

Early the next morning I pressed on. Driving across the Wisconsin prairie in the afternoon I watched thunderstorms gather force until I was in the midst of them, clinging to the steering wheel, trying to find the submerged road before me. Lightning struck all around me, and the rain flowed like a river down my windshield.

When I reached La Crosse, the final destination of my trip, I breathed a deep sigh. I was here to visit my son's grave, which I had last seen nearly ten years before, with my husband at my side. I began to cry and could not stop. I was barely intelligible to the friendly, hospitable man at the motel desk. I was so driven to reach the grave that I didn't stop to eat, to gain a bit of energy and compose myself.

With a town map, I located the large, old cemetery where five generations of my husband's family lie buried. The fifth generation is my son. Finding the office closed, I sat in the car for a few moments, trying to recollect the location of the grave. Then, as a migrating bird remembers the site of its previous year's nest, I moved slowly along the network of paths, among the tall trees and verdant shrubs, through the monuments and tombstones, until I found my husband's family's plot.

There it was, the small rectangle of polished granite bearing Peter's name and the years of his birth and death. I kneeled down and kissed the letters of his name. I talked to Peter and told him how much I loved him. I noticed for the first time how many young people lay in graves close to his, and that gave me comfort. I felt as if I were visiting Peter again, not just a plot in a vast cemetery of plots, but as if I were in his living presence. No one else was around in the cool of the evening, so I continued to talk. I remembered old times, told him again that I loved him.

I laid a red rose on his grave. A swell of longing overcame me in that June-green evening above the Mississippi—longing to be close, once more, to my living, breathing son. I looked at the trails of water that the rain had traced on Peter's gravestone and felt corresponding trails of tears staining my cheeks. Then all was quiet. I sat still a long time, admiring the freshness of the living rose on the polished gray stone.

I stood and took one last look at the final resting place of my son, then turned and left. I drove through the tall trees of the cemetery, through the straight streets of La Crosse, until I was out in the rolling hills of southwestern Wisconsin, sailing down empty roads, windows wide open, hair tousled beyond taming, eyes steady on the road ahead that led me farther and farther away from the grave of my son.

I decided to take the blue roads home, the back roads that link the towns, rather than the slick interstates that bypass all the communities. I had no plan for the return loop home, no deadlines of when I had to be where, and I don't like the high speeds on the interstates or the way people drive on them with blinders, looking neither right nor left, just aiming for their destination. I wanted to see how the people lived on the land. I took a break in a county park along the Wisconsin River, where monster mosquitoes drove me quickly back to the car. I stopped for a root beer in a small town, where I was served by a pretty car-hop. I read the signs marking the stores and shops in all the towns and spoke the names out loud.

With the sun at my back, I drove on to Fort Atkinson in south-eastern Wisconsin, where, with the help of local women, I found the home of a poet whose work I have admired. Lorine Niedecker once lived in the simplest setting, in what many would call poverty, on remote Black Hawk Island in the middle of Rock River. Every year the river floods the island, and every year she joined forces with her neighbors in the annual rite of staving off the swollen waters—often so high they invaded the cabin where she wrote.

Lorine Niedecker was born in this watery place in 1903, one year before my mother was born. She loved the river, the birds, the plant life. Her poems are condensed, filled with pithy observations of her life of solitude, her love of her home on the Rock River.

> Nobody, nothing
>   ever gave me
>   greater thing
>
> than time
>   unless light
>   and silence
>
> which if intense
>   makes sound

Perhaps I am attracted to Niedecker's work because it reminds me of the poems I wish my mother had written. As a girl, looking up to my mother with her knowledge and love of literature, I imagined that some day, when she had the time, she would write her own poetry. When my mother died, I found notebooks of poems copied out in her beautiful hand, but none that she had composed. Like many women of her generation and class, my mother filled her days with domestic routines, care of her ever-growing family and volunteer community service, leaving little time for self-expression. I hope whatever modest legacy of written words and music I leave behind will inspire my daughter to manifest her own abundant creativity.

The sign erected by the state of Wisconsin commemorated the home of Lorine Niedecker with the appraisal: her poems "ranked among the 20th century's finest." I smelled the dampness as I walked over the dark brown earth, leaving my footprints in the marsh mud. I looked at the trees standing in water, the paint peeling on the logs of her cabin, the bird's nest perched precariously on the top of a shutter. I touched the water pump, standing idle on the small front lawn. Then, hearing a commotion, I looked skyward and saw three sandhill cranes flying overhead, hooting their loud, rattling call in salute to the memory of the woman who understood them and heralded them in her poetry.

The next morning I was back on the back roads again, heading far south to bypass Chicago before turning east. I marveled at how straight the roads were, cutting through Illinois fields of corn that stretched to the horizon. The deep-green stalks were waist-high, and it was not yet the fourth of July. I drove on and on down the strips of roads, sipping iced tea as I drove, trying to stave off sleep in the summer afternoon. Only the silos stood out, erect in the blue sky.

Approaching Gilman, Illinois, the road took a right angle where I came upon the largest grain elevators I had ever seen. A whole group of them dwarfed a three-story wooden house to my left, and I slowed down to admire them, but not slow enough, for when my eyes returned to the road ahead, my car was bearing down on the back of a van. I slammed on the brakes as hard as I could, but not quickly enough to avoid plowing into the rear of the van. It was a surreal experience for me—the first accident I had had in forty-four years of driving. The shock of it posed the inevitable question: was I becoming old and careless?

When the policeman, whom the van driver had called, finally rolled up to our parked vehicles forty-five minutes later, he smiled sheepishly and apologized for his late arrival, explaining he had been in the bathtub when he had received our call. We filled out the required forms, and a local mechanic assured me the car was safe to drive home. As I shook hands with the van driver, a great-grand-mother who was younger than I, she wished me Godspeed and a safe trip; then returning to her van, she called out, "But I know it's too late to wish you a safe journey now."

Waking the following morning in a gaudy yellow motel too close to the road, I looked at a calendar and realized it was the beginning of the Fourth-of-July weekend. I decided to change course and take the nearest interstate so that I could return home to North Carolina by evening. After the accident the day before, I was caving in a bit to self-doubt. The voices of those people who had told me I shouldn't take such a long trip alone spun in my head. I had begun the trip wanting to prove to myself that I could still travel easily alone. Now I would return home with the front end of my car smashed in. It was not the way I had wanted it to be.

I left the two-lane roads behind and, with firm resolve, turned onto Interstate 75 South. Already the traffic was heavier than I had seen since Washington, D.C., and I wondered if I had made a mistake.

Suddenly the screech of brakes filled the air and in the same instant I saw a rock, bigger than a man's fist, coming at my wind-shield. I felt as if I were in a sci-fi film, watching a meteor hurtling toward my spacecraft. My windshield exploded, and glass splinters showered me as the rock fell onto my dashboard and then rolled to the floor, knocking over my iced tea. I was dazed, but held on

tight. The wind coming through the large hole in the windshield
blew more glass onto my face and neck. I had been driving at sev-
enty miles per hour in the left lane of the interstate, and now I
focused on finding a safe haven for my twice-wounded vehicle. I
pushed my way through the holiday traffic into the right lane and
then onto the right shoulder. When I finally brought the car to a
halt, I was trembling.

Sitting on the edge of the interstate with traffic roaring by, I
examined my face in the rearview mirror. It was speckled with
blood, and my hair was tangled with splinters of glass. I looked
down and saw that my hands, right arm and chest were coated with
cuts. Yesterday's accident, it turned out, was a mere foreshadowing
of today's. "I know it's too late to wish you a safe journey now," the
great-grandmother had said.

The police arrived, followed by an ambulance, whose team
cleaned me up and remarked more than once that most drivers, on
having a three-pound rock hit their windshield at high speed, would
have crashed. My car was towed to a junkyard in the country, and by
evening I was sitting on the front porch of a Kentucky hill family's
home, surrounded by dilapidated vehicles, drinking fresh iced tea
and meeting the members of a three-generation family with ten
grandchildren.

Three days I spent in that small Kentucky hill town with no car,
walking from the cheapest motel to eat my meals in a local home-
cookin' restaurant. Because of the holiday weekend, I would have
to wait until businesses reopened on Monday to get a new windshield. In the heat of the July afternoons I swam with the locals in
the motel pool. I ate chicken croquettes with mashed potatoes and
gravy for dinner and eggs and grits for breakfast. But it wasn't until
Sunday that I walked to the nearest church.

The Baptists took me in, and in one day I attended three church services and took my turn reading Bible verses in the women's Sunday School. I sang in the choir and listened while the entire congregation prayed not only for my safe arrival home, but for a "trouble-free trip." I witnessed a seven-year-old girl's baptism by total immersion after she had told her grandfather and the pastor and then the entire congregation, "I want to know God."

I listened to Pastor John's sonorous voice ring out in his sermon based on 2 Corinthians 3:5, "But our sufficiency is of God." Again and again, he came back to the thought that we are not sufficient unto ourselves, but our sufficiency comes from God. Sitting there in the wooden pew next to my newly made friends, I felt as if Pastor John were speaking directly to me, as if he were there to remind me that no matter how independent and self-sufficient I think I am, my life, my strength is derived from a higher power.

"Balance," I said to myself. The golden mean. How many times I have tried to understand the subtlety of balance. Whether it be between the spiritual and the temporal, between freedom and responsibility, work and play, travel and home, the masculine and feminine or the individual and the relationship, the good life is well balanced. There in the hills of Kentucky, in a little Baptist church where the gospel has been preached for nearly two hundred years, I thought again about balance, about how I had been striving these last ten years to be self-sufficient, but the truth is that I am inextricably connected to the world around me. I am surrounded by family and friends, even strangers, who help me along the way.

The January sun is shining full force, as if to give me a warm welcome home. I shift position on the ancient granite rock above my farmhouse and, feeling the winter wind, wrap my Nepalese cashmere scarf closer around my head. After travel it is good to be home—to sit by the woodstove on cold evenings, to have the time to read and to play my old Steinway piano, its deep resonance filling the rooms of the house with song. I take delight in my never-ending role of mother, following with interest the course of my daughter's life and continuing to honor the life of my son. Having completed my round-the-world journey and proven to myself, once again, that I can do things on my own, I am glad to share my life with the man I love.

After travel, it is time to settle in, to savor the beauty of my own hills, to reflect and to act. The challenge is to be awake and to awaken others to the positive possibilities for shaping our tomorrows.

Like the brown milkweed pod I see resting on its dry stalk, each moment contains the fruit of the past as well as the seeds for the future. It is left to us to bring the seeds of the moment to fruition in the warmth of our days.

Author photo: Thomas Crowe

Writer and musician Nan Watkins was born and raised in Bucks County, Pennsylvania. She holds degrees from Oberlin College and Johns Hopkins University and studied at the University of Munich and the Academy of Music in Vienna. A CD of her original music, *The Laugharne Poems,* was released in 1995. She has traveled throughout the world and her travel essays have appeared in *Hot Flashes from Abroad* and *A Woman Alone.* She works as a reference librarian at Western Carolina University and lives in Tuckasegee, North Carolina.

BOOKS

Dream of a Thousand Lives by Karen Connelly. $14.95, ISBN 1-58005-062-X.

A Woman Alone: Travel Tales from Around the Globe edited by Faith Conlon, Ingrid Emerick and Christina Henry de Tessan. $15.95, ISBN 1-58005-059-X.

The Unsavvy Traveler: Women's Comic Tales of Catastrophe edited by Rosemary Caperton, Anne Mathews and Lucie Ocenas, introduction by Pam Houston. $15.95, ISBN 1-58005-058-1.

Journey Across Tibet: A Young Woman's Trek Across the Rooftop of the World by Sorrel Wilby. $16.95, ISBN 1-58005-053-0.

Hot Flashes from Abroad: Women's Travel Tales and Adventures edited by Jean Gould. $16.95, ISBN 1-58005-055-7.

No Hurry to Get Home: The Memoir of the New Yorker *Writer Whose Unconventional Life and Adventures Spanned the Twentieth Century* by Emily Hahn. $14.95, ISBN 1-58005-045-X.

Pilgrimage to India: A Woman Revisits Her Homeland by Pramila Jayapal. $14.95, ISBN 1-58005-052-2.

Solo: On Her Own Adventure edited by Susan Fox Rogers. $12.95, ISBN 1-878067-74-5.

Expat: Women's True Tales of Life Abroad edited by Christina Henry de Tessan. $16.95, ISBN 1-58005-070-0

The Curve of Time by M. Wylie Blanchet. $15.95, ISBN 1-58005-072-7